THE AMERICAN BAR ASSOCIATION

GUIDE TO

RESOLVING LEGAL DISPUTES

INSIDE AND OUTSIDE THE COURTROOM

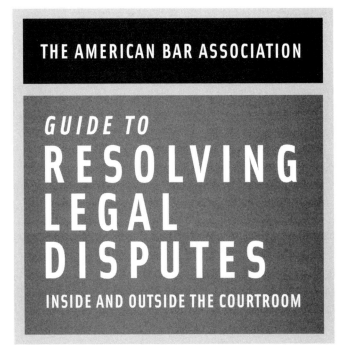

THE AMERICAN BAR ASSOCIATION

GUIDE TO
RESOLVING
LEGAL
DISPUTES

INSIDE AND OUTSIDE THE COURTROOM

RANDOM HOUSE REFERENCE

NEW YORK   TORONTO   LONDON   SYDNEY   AUCKLAND

Library of Congress Cataloging-in-Publication Data

The American Bar Association guide to resolving legal disputes : inside and outside the courtroom.
p.   cm.
ISBN 978-0-375-72141-0
1. Dispute resolution (Law)—United States—Popular works.   2. Attorney and client—United States—Popular works.   I. American Bar Association.
II. Title: Guide to resolving legal disputes.

KF9084.Z9A54 2007
347.73'9—dc22   2006050401

Visit the Random House Reference Web site: *www.randomwords.com*

Okianer Christian Dark
Howard University
School of Law
Washington, D.C.

William T. Hogan III
Nelson Mullins Riley
and Scarborough LLP
Boston, Massachusetts

Harry S. Johnson
Whiteford Taylor Preston
Baltimore, Maryland

Honorable Judith S. Kaye
Chief Judge of the State
of New York
New York, New York

Jill Suzanne Miller
Duke University
School of Law
Durham, North Carolina

Martin N. Olsen
Olsen & Olsen
Midvale, Utah

Gary Slaiman
Bingham McCutcheon LLP
Washington, D.C.

Bert Z. Tigerman
The Wartnick Law Firm
San Francisco, California

Mary T. Torres
Modrall Sperling
Roehl Harris et al
Albuquerque, New Mexico

Patricia D. White
Arizona State University
College of Law
Tempe, Arizona

CONTENTS

Foreword   xi
Introduction   xiii

1. An Introduction to Conflict   1
From Outbursts to Handshakes

2. Negotiation   18
Reaching Agreement Through Interest-Based Negotiation

3. Mediation   43
Three Heads are Better Than Two

4. Arbitration   67
A Flexible Alternative to Litigation

5. Small-Claims Court   93
The "Fast Food" of the Legal System

6. Court Procedures for Civil Cases   117
Understanding a Trial from Start to Finish

7. Finding and Working with a Lawyer   152
How to Find the Right Lawyer for Your Case

8. Where Do You Go from Here?   176
Our Top Recommendations for Further Resources

Index   179
About the Author   187

FOREWORD

Henry F. White Jr.
Executive Director, American Bar Association

When American families are asked to describe their legal needs, the topics that come up repeatedly are housing, personal finance, wills and estates, family and domestic concerns, and employment-related issues. The books in the *American Bar Association Legal Guide* series are designed to address these key legal areas, and provide information about the law in plain, direct language.

The goal of this book is to help you work with your lawyer to handle disputes, both inside and outside the courtroom. It provides information on the range of options that can be used in solving everyday legal problems, including negotiation, mediation and arbitration. We hope it will help you negotiate some of the legal issues that arise in specific disputes; we also hope that by removing much of the mystery from the legal system it will help you feel more comfortable with the law generally.

As the largest voluntary professional association in the world and the nation's premier source of legal information, the American Bar Association is in a unique position to provide insightful commentary on the law. The ABA also provides support for lawyer referral programs and pro bono services (for which lawyers donate their time), as it works to help make finding the right lawyer and receiving quality legal help an attainable goal for everyone.

This book was written with the aid of ABA members—including lawyers, judges, mediators, arbitrators, and academics—from across the country. Their contribution is invaluable. They have experience in dealing with legal disputes every day and their perspectives and expertise make this a better book.

The ABA's Standing Committee on Public Education provided oversight for this project. The programs, publications, and resources of the ABA Division for Public Education are designed to educate the public about the rule of law and help people understand and participate in our legal system. Public education and public service are two of the most important goals of the American Bar Association. Through publications, outreach, and our website (*www.abanet.org*), the ABA strives to provide accurate, unbiased legal information to our members, to the media, and to the general public.

Henry F. White Jr. is the Executive Director of the American Bar Association. He was formerly President of the Institute of International Container Lessors, the trade association for the worldwide container and chassis leasing industry, and is a retired Rear Admiral in the U.S. Navy.

INTRODUCTION

Dwight L. Smith, *Chair*
ABA Standing Committee on Public Education

Disputes inevitably arise between people in every part of the country, every day. Common disputes spring from employment, divorce or separation, automobile accidents, or arguments with a neighbor over a boundary line. Any dispute, large or small, can lead to frayed emotions and can take time, money, and patience to resolve.

When you think about resolving a dispute, you might think of a judge making a decision in a courtroom, perhaps as represented in a TV show or movie. However, only a tiny fraction of disputes end up in court. The Bureau of Justice Statistics at the U.S. Department of Justice estimates that only 3 percent of all civil cases end in a trial. The vast majority of disputes are resolved before they ever get to court.

Different disputes call for different kinds of resolutions, and this book provides an overview of the options. It illustrates the basic principles of negotiation, and includes tips on how you can improve your negotiating skills. It describes the various approaches to mediation, and outlines the mediation process. It includes information on arbitration and arbitrators, with special information for consumers. It explains the procedures of small claims courts, and gives tips on how to present a case in small claims court. It sketches the basics of civil court procedure, from discovery, to depositions, to your day in court. And it gives detailed information about how you can find and work with a lawyer, whether your dispute is large or small.

If you are involved in one of life's inevitable disputes, this book can help you decide which approach is best for resolving the problem. It can also help you identify and resolve conflicts before they become major problems.

WRITTEN AND REVIEWED BY EXPERTS

The principal author of this book is Sheila Maloney, a Clinical Assistant Professor of Law at the Northwestern University School of Law, and Assistant Director of the Law School's Program on Negotiation and Mediation. Her manuscript was intensively reviewed by ABA members from across the country who are experts in their fields. Members of the ABA's Section of Dispute Resolution took a particular interest in this project, as did members of the Dispute Resolution Committee of the National Conference of State Trial Judges. Their careful review assured that the manuscript accurately and thoroughly covered this important subject. We thank them for their interest and involvement.

The entire project was completed under the guidance of the ABA's Standing Committee on Public Education. Together, we've worked to provide you with easy-to-read information that will help you understand disputes and know how to handle them.

WRITTEN WITH YOU IN MIND

We've made a special effort to make this book practical, by using situations and problems you are likely to encounter. You won't find legal jargon or technicalities here—just concise, straightforward discussions of your options under the law. Within chapters, you'll find sidebars with the following icons:

- ▶, which share practical tips that could be of benefit to you;
- ⓘ, which signal key additional information;
- ⚠, which warn you about potential pitfalls that you can navigate with the right information and help;
- ▤, which give clear, plain English definitions to legal terms;

- ( ), which highlight experts' responses to practical questions, giving legal information that may help you as you grapple with similar issues within your own family.

You'll find two additional features at the end of each chapter:

- "The World at Your Fingertips," which contains tips on where to go for more information if you'd like to explore a topic further.

- "Remember This," which highlights the most important points that the chapter has covered.

One word of caution: when reading this book, and other books in the series, remember that these books cannot and do not purport to provide legal advice. Only a lawyer can apply the law to the unique facts of your particular case. Although every effort has been made to present material that is as up-to-date as possible, laws can and do change. Laws can also vary widely from one jurisdiction to the next. If you are thinking about pursuing legal action, you should consult with a lawyer. To find one, contact your local bar association or lawyer referral service.

With that in mind, this book can help you make informed decisions about a wide range of problems and options. Armed with the knowledge and insights this book provides, you can be confident that the decisions you make will be in your best interest.

Dwight Smith is chair of the ABA's Standing Committee on Public Education and is an attorney in private practice in Tulsa, Oklahoma. A significant portion of his practice is devoted to dispute resolution.

CHAPTER 1

An Introduction to Conflict

From Outbursts to Handshakes

Two children in a playground fight over a ball.

A union representative meets with management to discuss wage increases.

A teenager argues with her parents about her curfew.

A woman tries to return a dress because the zipper is broken.

State legislators battle over a zoning ordinance.

One driver sues another for injuries resulting from a car accident.

A teacher speaks with a parent about expelling a child from school.

Two company representatives meet to discuss a shipment of goods that was destroyed by fire.

While these scenarios differ in scope, they all involve conflict of some kind. In fact, conflict is all around us, whether we are at home, at work, or in the marketplace.

For most people, the term "conflict" has negative connotations. We tend to associate disagreements or heated discussions with broken relationships, confusion, anger, and frustration. However, conflict doesn't have to be negative. If it didn't produce positive results, we wouldn't engage in conflict so often. When properly employed, conflict can serve as a catalyst for opening lines of communication and improving relationships. That's why we feel good after we reconcile with a friend or partner after an argument; conflict can help clear the air and help people learn something new in the process.

While there is no perfect process for resolving all disputes, there are ways to resolve disputes and manage conflicts to achieve positive results. The more we understand our own disputes and what drives them, the better equipped we are to resolve them effectively.

This book provides an overview of the options available for resolving disputes. This chapter outlines five methods of conflict resolution: negotiation, mediation, arbitration, small-claims court, and litigation (i.e., filing a lawsuit). Subsequent chapters of this book explore the pros and cons of each of these processes. We will consider when it is appropriate to negotiate or go to court; when you should mediate rather than arbitrate; the advantages and disadvantages of resolving disputes in small-claims courts and other state and federal courts; when you should hire a lawyer; and how you can work with a lawyer most effectively. At the end of this book, you will be in a better position to decide which approach is best for handling your conflict.

Keep one simple rule in mind as you read this book: The less formal the procedure used to resolve your dispute, the more control you will have over the final outcome and cost. For example, in a negotiation, you have a great deal of control over the cost, process, and outcome. A lawsuit is at the other end of the spectrum; it allows you much less control over each of these factors.

NEGOTIATION

Negotiation has existed for as long as humans have had the ability to communicate. Everyone—from small children deciding who goes first in a game of kickball, to heads of state discussing international disputes—negotiates in some capacity.

Many of us have engaged in a legal negotiation at some point in our lives. What does a legal negotiation look like? Suppose, for example, that Nelma and John buy a condominium. After they have settled in, they discover that the chimney doesn't work and requires repairs costing $5,000. They consider various options, including suing the previous owner and the inspector they hired prior to their closing. But they don't want to incur the expense of going to court. Instead, they decide to discuss the issue with the previous owner in an attempt to work things out. That discussion is a negotiation. After an initial meeting, Nelma,

NEGOTIATION

According to the Merriam-Webster Dictionary, to **negotiate** is "to confer with another so as to arrive at the settlement of some matter." Essentially, negotiation occurs when two or more people bargain for what they want.

John, and the former owner might work out a plan to redesign the chimney, which adds value to the condo for Nelma and John. The owner might offer a discount for the redesign, and the parties might decide to split the cost of the repair between them. A successful negotiation can help the parties avoid a lawsuit.

Most adults negotiate every day. Negotiations can be simple unstructured conversations, or they can be more formal. As people negotiate, they may reach an agreement, choose to continue negotiating, or end the process altogether. Negotiations offer great flexibility in this regard—parties are free to negotiate an issue as far as they wish, and can walk away without investing a great deal of time or money if they cannot reach agreement.

If two parties successfully negotiate, they may choose to formalize any agreement they reach in a written contract. This is common in a business negotiation where contract terms or a salary are being negotiated. However, not all successful negotiations end in a written contract. For instance, if you are purchasing a bicycle from a yard sale, you might agree to a price, money may change hands, and you might ride the bike home—all without ever signing a contract. Similarly, if a group of tenants in an office building negotiates a 10 percent employee discount with a local coffee shop, a contract is probably unnecessary.

Negotiation is a natural first step in resolving a dispute. It provides opportunities to correct mistakes and save relationships that may be destroyed if lawsuits are filed. In addition, negotiation usually offers a broad range of solutions. One reason for

▶ **SILENCE IS GOLDEN**

The 1940 movie *Edison, the Man* chronicles the life of famed inventor Thomas Edison. In one scene, Edison illustrates the power of silence in a negotiation. When he goes into a meeting to sell an invention, he says very little—he lets the buyer make the first offer and take the lead in the negotiation. At the end of the meeting, the two sides agree on a price of $40,000. The buyer says, "It might interest you to know that I would have gone as high as $60,000." Edison smiles and replies, "It would interest you to know that I was planning to sell it for $2,000."

this is that, when people negotiate, they tend not only to focus on their own interests, but also to seek ways of accommodating the interests of others. Good negotiators are more interested in achieving a favorable outcome than in proving who is right or wrong.

Chapter 2 of this book provides information about how to prepare for negotiation effectively, and how to negotiate based on interests rather than positions. It also provides information about why negotiations sometimes break down, and how you can avoid common negotiating pitfalls.

MEDIATION

Another way to resolve a conflict is through mediation. **Mediation** is negotiation that is facilitated by a neutral third party, the mediator.

A simple example from the workplace can illustrate the mechanics of the mediation process and some of its advantages. Suppose Tracy has worked at her current job for sixteen years. According to performance reviews, her job performance has always ranged from average to good. But then she is passed over for a promotion, and the promotion is given to Simone, who has been at the company for only four years. When Tracy asks her supervisor why she missed out on the promotion, she is told that the company wanted "younger, more energetic people" on the management team.

Tracy talks to a lawyer about her options. On her lawyer's recommendation, she files a claim with the Equal Employment Opportunity Commission (EEOC) alleging that her company discriminated against her because of her age. The company denies the charge, claiming that Tracy's supervisor misrepresented company policy. It claims that Tracy was passed over because of her substandard performance and lack of commitment to the company. The EEOC refers the case to mediation.

Tracy's lawyer and the company's human resources director, Quincy, select a neutral mediator. Tracy attends the mediation with her lawyer, and Quincy also attends. The mediator begins by setting ground rules for discussion and explaining the mediation process. She tells the parties that they can discuss whatever issues they want, and encourages them to listen to one another. To facilitate the discussion, the mediator meets with the parties together, and also meets with each party separately.

In the course of the mediation, Tracy learns about the promotion process and how candidates for promotion are selected. She learns of Simone's many accomplishments, about which she hadn't previously known. Quincy listens to Tracy and learns that many of the company's older employees are nervous about being replaced or passed over for younger workers. He acknowledges that management has not been proactive enough in informing all employees about opportunities for promotion within the company. After several hours, the parties reach a confidential agreement: Tracy will be given more responsibility on some projects, which will enhance her eligibility for future promotions. Quincy will set up a staff group to address the concerns of employees over fifty, and will ensure that older employees are included in all company training sessions.

Before the mediation, Tracy was mistrustful of management. Quincy was disappointed that a complaint had been made

( ) TALKING TO A LAWYER

Q. *Are there any disputes that are not suitable for mediation? I'm getting a divorce, and my ex wants to mediate the issue of child custody. But I feel that he always bullies me, and I'm very nervous about the mediation process.*

A. A case is unsuitable for mediation when one or both parties are unable to negotiate in their own best interests, or have agreed to mediation under duress or coercion.

Divorce mediation should only be conducted by a mediator trained to screen clients for impediments to mediation, such as a history of domestic violence, substance abuse, or mental illness. The presence of one of these factors does not automatically render a case inappropriate for mediation, but the mediator must take precautionary measures to assure as safe a mediation as possible. No mediator can guarantee total safety, but mediators can follow certain guidelines to facilitate a safe experience.

Ideally, prior to a divorce or family mediation, the parties should meet individually with the mediator to discuss any safety concerns. A divorce or family mediator can employ a wide variety of tactics to make parties feel more comfortable during a mediation, such as encouraging each party to bring along a support person or attorney; **shuttle mediating** (in which the parties occupy separate rooms, with the mediator shuttling back and forth between them); providing separate waiting rooms, so that the parties are never alone together outside of the mediator's presence; and **co-mediation** (i.e., use of two mediators) in which both a male and female mediator are present in the room to provide a gender balance.

Whenever possible, divorcing parties should have legal representation during a mediation. Ordinarily, parties do not sign any agreements during a divorce mediation, especially when their attorneys are not in the room. If the parties reach agreement, the mediator will record the agreement in writing for them. Sometimes this written summary of the agreement is called a **memorandum of understanding**. The parties should take the written agreement back to their attorneys for review and counsel. If the parties wish to have the agreement enforced, their attorneys will formalize the agreement by writing it up in legal language, and will submit it to a judge for his or her approval. When signed by a judge, the agreement will become a court order which is then enforceable by the court.

—Answer by Cookie Levitz, mediator,
Chicago, Illinois

about the company, and was convinced that Tracy was a troublemaker. With the help of a mediator, however, both sides were able to see that their opinions were the result of misunderstandings, and that in fact they had a common interest in the company. By talking with each other, they were able to resolve the dispute to their mutual satisfaction.

This example demonstrates several benefits of mediation. For one thing, a mediator has the ability to suggest a broad range of possible solutions, because he or she has no stake in the outcome, and no incentive to favor one position over another. The mediator is also able to bring a cool head to the table and facilitate a discussion by asking questions. However, the parties themselves are ultimately in control of the agreement reached, if an agreement is reached at all.

Disputing parties may arrange for formal mediation through a private agency, a workplace ombudsman service, or a community mediation service. In some cases, mediation may be ordered by a court.

Mediation is a convenient means of resolving many common disputes, including workplace disputes, disagreements between neighbors, disputes relating to issues of family custody, and disputes regarding business matters. Sometimes mediation is appropriate if parties have reached an impasse in their attempts to negotiate; a mediator is an appropriate next step if you want to continue talking, but are unable to do so productively on your own. In addition, mediation is cheaper, faster, and offers a broader range of settlement options than a traditional trial. It may also allow you to have a more engaging experience with the other side than would a "day in court."

In a mediation, the parties normally share the cost of the mediator. In many regions, parties can obtain free or sliding-scale mediation at community centers. The costs of mediation are higher than the costs of negotiation, because mediation involves a third person, but the costs are typically less than those of either arbitration or litigation.

Chapter 3 of this book provides additional information about the types of disputes that are commonly mediated, the advantages and disadvantages of mediation, and the extent to which mediators typically play a part in dispute resolution. You can learn more about the credentials that you should consider when selecting a mediator, explore what happens when mediation fails, and learn what dispute resolution options are appropriate in the event of such a failure.

ⓘ MEDIATION IN SCHOOLS

You may already know that mediation is an effective tool that sophisticated litigants can use to resolve disputes. But did you also know that mediation is growing increasingly popular in high schools? Some high schools select and train students as peer mediators to facilitate discussions between students in order to resolve disagreements. Generally, school officials decide which disputes are appropriate for peer mediation.

Mediation gives students the opportunity to engage in dialogue about their disputes, and to work toward solving the underlying problems. Teens involved in peer mediation report that they feel empowered to solve their own problems. In addition, schools that use peer mediators note that students are much more open and comfortable discussing their problems with peers than with adult authority figures.

( ) TALKING TO A LAWYER

Q. I believe that my employer fired me because I'm over fifty-five. I hired a lawyer, who says that if I mediate the issue with my employer I may be able to get my job back, and possibly some money. But what I really want to do is make sure that my employer never fires another employee because of his or her age. Can I achieve this result through mediation?

A. Absolutely. An enormous benefit of mediation is that it can be a very creative process, allowing for many different kinds of resolutions that can be custom-tailored to the specific needs and interests of the parties. As long as your employer agrees to what you want and can actually follow through on it, you can create an enforceable agreement. Of course, a mediated agreement cannot violate any laws.

—Answer by Cookie Levitz,
mediator, Chicago, Illinois

ARBITRATION

In **arbitration**, the parties to a dispute agree to a private hearing with an arbitrator or an arbitration panel. The **arbitrator** is an impartial third party who listens to the details of a dispute by the parties, considers all evidence presented, and issues a decision. In **binding arbitration**, the parties agree in advance to be bound by the arbitrator's decision, which is enforceable in a court of law. In **nonbinding arbitration**, the arbitrator's opinion is only advisory. This means that the parties may agree to adhere to the advisory opinion, settle the case under different terms, or decide to continue with litigation.

The arbitrator controls the process during an arbitration hearing, which is similar to a trial, although the rules of evidence that apply to court proceedings generally do not apply to arbitration. The arbitrator decides the outcome in a role similar

( ) TALKING TO A LAWYER

Q. A friend of mine told me that arbitration is a bad idea, because it doesn't offer the protections of a court or judge, and the parties end up with a decision that they can't appeal. Is this true?

A. No, it's not true that arbitration is a bad idea. It *might* be true that there will be no court, judge, or right to appeal—but those facts do not necessarily mean that arbitration is a bad idea. In fact, the absence of a right to appeal is generally regarded as the most important benefit of arbitration. Binding arbitration, which results in a decision that you can't appeal, is almost always the result of an agreement by the parties. Sometimes a person can unintentionally agree to arbitrate if he or she signs a contract without reading the "fine print." But in most cases, arbitration comes about because the parties actively agree to it.

When agreeing to arbitrate, the parties can agree on the conditions of the arbitration, such as the number of arbitrators, the means by which arbitrators will be selected, the qualifications that arbitrators must have, whether or not **discovery** (pretrial investigation) will be permitted before the arbitration hearing, the extent to which the arbitrator(s) will have authority to order compliance with discovery requests, and the manner in which the arbitration hearing(s) will be scheduled and conducted. By agreeing to binding arbitration, the parties agree to accept the decision of the arbitrator(s), thus definitively resolving the dispute in a manner that is generally cheaper and faster than a lawsuit. If you lose an arbitration, it may be tempting to think that you would have done better if you had gone to court. But in fact, there may be no real basis for that belief.

One other point worth noting is that, in some jurisdictions where the court will cooperate, the parties can agree that disputed points of law arising before the arbitration hearing can be resolved by a panel of judges rather than by the arbitrators. One weakness of binding arbitration can be that the arbitrator is the final word on both the law and the facts of your case. This means that if the arbitrator is not legally trained, the parties may ultimately feel that the arbitrator rendered inaccurate rulings on points of law. Of course, one side or the other is probably going to feel this way even if the arbitrator *is* legally trained—but that would be the result even if the parties had gone to court.

The bottom line: If you agree to binding arbitration, be careful about the process by which the arbitrator or arbitrators are picked, and the qualifications that the arbitrators must possess, such as legal training.

—Answer by Judge Robert Shenkin,
Court of Common Pleas of Chester County,
West Chester, Pennsylvania

to that of a judge. Unlike court proceedings, arbitration is held in a closed and private court, and the parties can keep the outcome confidential.

Arbitration is very popular in certain industries. For example, arbitration has a long and rich history as a means of resolving labor disputes. In addition, many of us are familiar with the use of arbitrators in sports. Arbitration is attractive in these and other commercial contexts because it allows disputes to be resolved more quickly than they would be resolved in court. In addition, unlike negotiation or mediation, arbitration can provide final, binding resolution and closure for the involved parties. The cost of arbitration is usually lower than the cost of a trial; however, the cost of arbitration has been increasing and the process can be quite expensive, depending on the individual arbitrator or company involved.

Chapter 4 of this book provides more detailed information about the arbitration process: how it works, the kinds of disputes that are usually arbitrated, and some issues of which consumers and employees need to be particularly aware.

SMALL-CLAIMS COURT

Small-claims courts are usually part of the state court system. In most small-claims courts, individuals can sue only to collect

(i) JUDGE JUDY IS REALLY ARBITRATOR JUDY

While many of us like to think of television's Judge Judy as a judge, she is actually an arbitrator (i.e., her cases are real, but she doesn't sit in a court), and her show provides an example of arbitration.

money. In addition, as the term "small claims" implies, people can only bring small cases to small-claims court; in most states, people may only bring cases worth a few thousand dollars or less. Typical small-claims disputes include landlord-tenant disputes, home repair complaints, and suits involving minor property damage.

You do not necessarily need a lawyer to bring a case in small-claims court. In fact, there are some states in which legal representation in small-claims court is not permitted. Being able to resolve a small legal case without hiring a lawyer can save you money. Most small-claims courts have clerks or other court employees who can help you with the procedures.

But just because you don't need a lawyer, you should not assume that your case will be easy. You should only represent yourself in a small-claims procedure if you are willing to invest some time and effort in your case. If you act as your own lawyer, you may need to do research, gather documents, and investigate

(i) A COURT BY ANY OTHER NAME

All states have special courts in which people can sue to collect small sums of money, but such courts have different names in different regions. Most are called **small-claims courts**, but some are called **magistrate courts**, **justice of the peace courts**, or **pro se courts**.

factual matters to prepare and present your case clearly and concisely.

Small-claims court procedures are similar to those of regular courts. The person initiating the lawsuit (the **plaintiff**) is generally required to file a complaint against the party from whom he or she seeks money. A judge or clerk will then set a date for a hearing, and the person being sued (the **defendant**) must be notified. At the hearing, both sides have a chance to present

( ) TALKING TO A LAWYER

Q. I paid a general contractor $5,000 to perform renovation work that he never performed. I won a case against him in small-claims for $5,000, but he hasn't paid me yet. What can I do?

A. In most cases, you can have a judgment entered against the contractor. You can then have your local sheriff serve a writ of execution. If the contractor has any assets, you can have those assets sold at a sheriff's sale. You will then get the proceeds from the sale, up to the amount of your judgment.

Unfortunately, many defendants (such as contractors) have no assets upon which a sheriff can issue a levy. The reason may be that the defendant is a corporation without assets. Or, if the defendant is an individual, his or her assets may be in the name of another person, such as a spouse, or held jointly with a spouse in a form of ownership that prevents a judgment creditor such as yourself from executing on those assets. Sometimes the ancient legal principle "you can't get blood from a stone" prevails, and you will be unable to get any money from the contractor even though you won in court. In that case, you will have received a very valuable but expensive education, and will know to protect yourself against similar situations in the future.

—Answer by Judge Robert Shenkin,
Court of Common Pleas of Chester County,
West Chester, Pennsylvania

their version of the story and produce evidence to help them argue their case.

In small-claims court, as in any court, the judge controls the process. After both sides have presented evidence, the judge will make a decision and either deliver it orally to the parties or mail it to them soon after the trial. The procedure is public, which means that anyone can attend.

Chapter 5 of this book will provide guidelines for determining whether your dispute is appropriate for small-claims court. It will also provide information about how to prepare for a small-claims suit, whether you are the plaintiff or the defendant.

THE COURT SYSTEM

There are two main types of legal trials in the United States: criminal trials and civil trials. In most states, criminal courts hear criminal trials, and civil courts hear civil trials; in some states, however, one court hears both kinds of cases. In criminal trials, defendants are accused of committing crimes that are punishable by fines and/or time in jail. In civil trials, individuals or companies bring lawsuits against other individuals or companies, in which they generally seek money as compensation for some kind of injury or wrong. In a criminal trial, the state or government brings an action on behalf of a victim. In a civil trial, private parties sue each other. One thing America learned from the infamous O.J. Simpson trial is that a person may be found not guilty in a criminal trial, but still be held accountable financially in a civil trial. This book will focus on the civil court system.

Parties in the trial system usually are represented by lawyers, and pay their own lawyer's fees even if they win the case (though there are some types of cases in which the winners are entitled to reimbursement of their attorney's fees). A civil case may be decided by a jury, but most trials are decided by judges. Before trial, each side seeks information from the other side in order to prepare its case adequately. This process can involve reading and preparing files of documents, interviewing witnesses, and hiring experts to analyze the evidence. Preparations for trial can take years.

At a trial, the plaintiff's and defendant's lawyers make opening statements, ask questions of witnesses, and produce documents and other physical objects as evidence. The judge or jury then weighs the evidence and makes a decision in favor of one party or the other.

From the date of filing to the rendering of a decision, a trial may take years. This is one of the largest drawbacks of litigation for many parties. For example, a simple breach-of-contract case between two corporations may take several years from start to finish. A complex lawsuit involving multiple plaintiffs and defendants can take more than a decade to resolve.

If you ask someone who has been through a court case about his or her experience in court, you will often get a negative reaction. Why is that? For one thing, the costs of going to court are rising; legal fees can quickly add up, and can rival or even surpass the sums at issue in the dispute. In addition, anyone who has been involved in litigation will tell you that the nonmonetary costs can also take their toll. Court dates require time off from work. Answering questions from the other side's attorney during a deposition can be painful and difficult. And waiting years for a case to be resolved can take an emotional toll. Finally, the powers of a court are limited. A civil court may award monetary compensation, but cannot provide the kinds of flexible solutions that you see in mediated or negotiated agreements. Tellingly, parties involved in litigation with one another often damage their relationship permanently.

These days, it should come as no surprise that litigation is usually a last resort for people who have tried negotiation and mediation and have been unable to reach agreement. In fact, lawyers often say that up to 95 percent of disputes are resolved or settled before they ever reach court.

Of course, in some cases a lawsuit may be the best means of resolving a dispute. Court decisions can have a broad reach, affecting situations and parties outside of your own case. For example, suppose you are fired from work for a reason that you think is unfair—for example, because of your sexual orientation. If you go to mediation with your employer and reach a confidential resolution, that outcome will be limited to you and your employer. Even if your employer agrees not to discriminate against other employees on the basis of sexual orientation, the results of your mediation will have no effect on other employers in your state. However, if you go to court and win, the outcome of your case can be used as legal precedent in similar disputes in your jurisdiction. This means that the case may be cited as grounds for preventing your employer and other employers from firing anyone else on the basis of sexual orientation. Of course, there is always a risk that you will lose the case. In this example, if a court were to determine that it is lawful to fire employees on the basis of sexual orientation, then your employer and other employers could continue firing people on that basis.

Chapter 6 of this book explains the litigation process in more depth, and provides more information about how to decide whether your dispute is right for litigation.

THE WORLD AT YOUR FINGERTIPS

• The website of the American Bar Association (ABA) Section of Dispute Resolution, at *www.abanet.org/dispute/resources.html*, includes information on a variety of dispute resolution programs and publications, from online dispute resolution to dispute resolution of tax matters.

• For an overview of mediation, news about dispute resolution, and a state-by-state directory of mediators, visit *www.mediate.com*.

• The website of the American Arbitration Association, at *www.adr.org*, offers a wide array of resources for those considering arbitration and/or mediation, including forms, information about procedures, and links to arbitrators and mediators.

• You can find more information about how courts work at the website of the ABA Division for Public Education, at *www.abanet.org/publiced/courts/home.html*.

REMEMBER THIS

- Conflict is not always a negative experience—it can help people communicate better and improve relationships in the long term.
- The less formal the procedure used to resolve a dispute, the more control the parties will have over the outcome and cost.
- If you are involved in a legal dispute, negotiation may be a natural first step for resolving it. Simply talking to the other party can often help to resolve a dispute, with no need for pursuing formal legal action.
- If your attempt to resolve a conflict through negotiation fails, you may wish to pursue mediation. Mediation is relatively informal and inexpensive, and can lead to creative solutions.
- Arbitration is more formal and usually more expensive than mediation, but less formal and expensive than going to court. Many contracts—such as employment contracts and contracts for home renovation—specify that arbitration must be used in the event of a dispute.
- Small-claims courts are special courts in which parties can bring cases and pursue small amounts of money. You can appear in small-claims court without a lawyer, but you will have to invest some time in preparing your case.
- If you have a dispute that can't be resolved any other way, you may wish to go to civil court. Litigation is expensive and time-consuming, and there's always going to be a winner and a loser. But on the upside, court decisions are immensely powerful; they can help change the law.

CHAPTER 2

Negotiation

Reaching Agreement Through Interest-Based Negotiation

Sam is an amateur poker player. Last year, he borrowed $10,000 from Geoff to play in the World Poker Series. Sam agreed to pay back the $10,000 to Geoff, regardless of whether he won any money. Moreover, he told Geoff, "If I win, I'll take care of you."

After an amazing display of skill and luck, Sam won it all at the World Poker Series, taking home a $1 million first prize. Sam promptly paid Geoff his $10,000, and gave him an additional gift of $15,000.

However, Geoff is not happy with $25,000. After all, it was his $10,000 that allowed Sam to play in the first place, and Sam specifically said that he would "take care" of Geoff if he won. Geoff demands that Sam pay him $100,000, which is only 10 percent of the money he won, or face a $500,000 lawsuit.

Sam doesn't want to get involved in a lawsuit, and he certainly doesn't want to end a long-standing friendship with Geoff. He decides to negotiate with Geoff to see if they can work out a deal.

Negotiation is the process of communicating with another person in order to reach agreement about something in which you both have an interest. If you have ever bought a car, asked for a raise, or argued over what movie to see, you have negotiated. In fact, we engage in negotiations every day, so this chapter is about a topic with which you already have some experience.

Although everyone has negotiated in some way, most people haven't had any formal training on how to prepare for or conduct a negotiation. When it comes to negotiating, far too many people simply wing it—including people who negotiate for a living, such as real estate agents. In her book *The Mind and Heart of the Negotiator*, Leigh Thompson documents studies demonstrating that even the most experienced businesspeople consistently fail to achieve the best possible results in negotiations. This chapter will help you understand and better prepare for negotiations, particularly those that take place in the context of a legal dispute. When it comes to negotiating, it's all about preparation. The more time you put into getting ready, the better the outcome you will achieve.

SHOULD YOU NEGOTIATE?

Your first decision is whether or not to negotiate at all. Negotiating almost always makes sense as a first step in resolving any dispute. Negotiating makes particular sense when both parties stand to benefit from an agreement. If each side has something or is capable of doing something that will satisfy the interests of the other side, both sides have a stake in meeting those mutual interests through negotiation. For instance, imagine Phil claims that Rosemary owes him $2,000 for a landscaping job he completed for her. Rosemary has the money to pay Phil, and acknowledges that she owes Phil some money, but she disagrees as to the amount. In this case, negotiating makes sense. Rosemary and Phil have a common interest in reaching agreement: Rosemary has money, and Phil has the ability to take Rosemary to court or to damage her reputation if she does not pay him.

Sometimes we become involved in disputes—monetary or otherwise—that are simply not worth our time. At one time or another we have all said to ourselves, "I should have just let that go." When deciding whether or not to negotiate, you should conduct a preliminary cost-benefit analysis of the situation. Ask yourself if the benefits of moving forward outweigh the costs in terms of time, money, and other resources.

Of course, some disputes may not be suitable for negotiation, such as family disputes in situations involving domestic violence.

( ) TALKING TO A LAWYER

Q. I'm involved in a dispute with my employer about my right to leave to care for my sick child. My employer wants to sit down and have a "negotiation session." Do I need a lawyer to help me?

A. Yes. Before negotiating, you need to know your legal rights, and to find out what will happen if your negotiations are not successful. You won't necessarily want your lawyer to come with you to the negotiating session, or even to let your employer know that you have consulted with a lawyer. (By the way, you can be sure that your employer has consulted with an attorney.) But in order to have a successful negotiating session, you will have to be clear about the outcome you want (your **target**) and the minimum you are willing to accept (your **reservation point**). Since you can't really determine a reasonable target and reservation point without knowing what will likely happen if you and your employer can't agree, you should consult with a lawyer to help you determine this information.

—Answer by Judge Robert Shenkin,
Court of Common Pleas of Chester County,
West Chester, Pennsylvania

Other situations call for increased caution—and possibly the assistance of a skilled negotiator, such as a lawyer—when approaching the negotiating table.

Parties who have proven to be dishonest or untrustworthy should be approached with caution. Suppose that Merlin enters into an agreement with Chris, a local mechanic, to rebuild the engine of his vintage BMW for $1,400. Chris promises to have the car ready in two weeks, but in fact takes more than three months to make the repairs. After Chris rebuilds the engine, the car runs for only two weeks before the engine explodes. Merlin is angry, but attempts to negotiate an agreement in order to get Chris to repay the $1,400. Chris promises he will pay $200 to

▶ **SEEK INDEPENDENT ADVICE**

Before making the decision to negotiate, consider consulting an independent advisor, such as a lawyer, to learn more about negotiating and
other dispute resolution options—particularly if the dispute is serious or
involves a significant amount of money. If you decide to negotiate, a
lawyer or other advisor can also assist you in preparing for and even conducting negotiations.

Merlin each month for seven months. Merlin does not feel entirely comfortable with the agreement because Chris has lied to
him before, but he hopes to settle the dispute as easily as possible. In this case, trusting Chris turns out to be a mistake. Chris
never makes any payments to Merlin; instead, he closes his shop
and moves out of the state.

Merlin could have recognized the danger of negotiating with
Chris, because Chris had already lied repeatedly about when the
car would be ready and about the quality of his services. Merlin
should have consulted a lawyer before negotiating. With good
advice, Merlin might have skipped the effort to negotiate and/or
initiated a lawsuit against Chris to secure a judgment ordering
Chris to repay him.

PREPARING FOR A NEGOTIATION

Once you have decided to negotiate a dispute, you should begin
to prepare for the negotiation. There is no substitute for preparation when it comes to negotiating effectively. The more you prepare, the more control you will have over the outcome. Before
entering into any negotiation, conduct the pre-negotiation assessment set forth below. It can be useful in any context, whether
you are negotiating in the boardroom or at a garage sale.

Self-Assessment

In preparing for a negotiation, the first thing you need to do is accurately assess where you stand going into it. As part of this process, it is important to consider all the issues that matter to you. Be sure you understand what you want from the negotiation. If you are trying to remedy harassment at work, for example, do you care about continuing with the job, or do you just want a monetary settlement? Be aware of why you want the result you're pursuing, and of your priorities. Is it important to you that the company conduct harassment training for all supervisors? Is it important that the company publicly apologize? What are your alternatives if the negotiation fails? Whatever your dispute, thinking about these types of questions can help you prepare for a successful negotiation.

Determine Your Interests

The first step in preparing for a negotiation is determining what result you want. The result you want determines your **position**, or point of view, during the negotiation. Your position will probably reflect the desire for a particular outcome. For example, your position in a salary negotiation might be, "I want more money."

Once you've established *what* you want from a negotiation, ask yourself *why* you want that result. The term **interest** refers to your personal stake in the outcome of a negotiation; your motivation to negotiate on your own behalf will be a reflection of your interests. Your interests are broader than your positions—they include your needs, desires and goals. In the case of a salary negotiation, for example, you might want more money because you've just had a new baby. Your interests include your desire to ensure a secure financial future for your child. When you are negotiating for your raise based on your interests (long-term financial security), your negotiation will be more fruitful. You may be willing to accept an employer savings plan or a long-term incremental increase rather than demanding more money now. Or you might decide to discuss advancement opportunities and how you can position yourself to achieve them. The bottom line is that when you negotiate solely on positions, such as "I want more money," you fail to recognize what is really driving your negotiation. People get more favorable results—from their negotiations and from their relationships in general—when they negotiate based on their interests rather than their positions.

For example, suppose that Sue is an accountant and Emily owns an office supply store. Sue asks Emily to create customized stationery for her office. When Sue fills out the order form for her stationery, she makes an error, which Emily then incorporates into the final print. Because the stationery features a mistake, it is useless. Sue asks Emily to reprint the stationery free of charge, but Emily refuses. Emily thinks that the error was Sue's fault, because Sue initially made the error when she filled out the form. Sue thinks that Emily should have given her an opportunity to proofread the stationery before the print run. Emily debits Sue's credit card for $3,000, the cost of the stationery. Sue then files a lawsuit against Emily seeking to recover that amount.

Sue's position is that she wants her money back. Emily's position is that she will not refund the money. When we look only at the *position* of each party, it appears that there are only three possible outcomes to their dispute: (1) Sue gets back the entire amount in dispute, (2) Sue gets back part of the amount in dispute, or (3) Sue gets back none of the amount in dispute.

However, examining the parties' *interests* reveals that their options for resolving the dispute are not nearly so limited. Sue's main interest is obtaining stationery for her business. Emily's interests include not going to court, not setting a precedent of providing unwarranted refunds, and preventing Sue from bad-mouthing her business. Both women have long-term interests in the success of their businesses. For Emily and Sue, the key to a successful negotiation is to examine these interests, and then generate options for settlements that will satisfy the interests of both parties. Emily does not want to reprint the stationery for free or give Sue a refund. However, if Sue agrees to buy stationery from Emily in the future if the reprint is successful, then Emily might be willing to reconsider; she might even reprint for free, or at a substantially discounted rate. Securing Sue's repeat business and a good reputation is probably worth more to Emily than the cost of the one reprint in dispute. In another possible outcome, Sue could provide accounting services to Emily's stationery business at a reduced rate in exchange for stationery products. Sue and Emily could also create a mutual referral agreement, in which Sue could agree to refer her customers to Emily's business, and vice versa. If Sue and Emily only negotiated based on their positions, they would lose opportunities for such creative solutions.

Determine Your BATNA

Once you assess your interests, you should determine your **best alternative to a negotiated agreement**, or **BATNA**. To determine your BATNA, ask yourself: "If negotiations don't work out, what will I do? What is my best course of action if negotiations fail?" For example, if negotiation fails to resolve a dispute, your BATNA might be pursuing the matter in small-claims court, or giving up the claim entirely.

Realistically determining your next-best option to a successful negotiation can provide a real incentive to make negotiations work. If all of your alternatives to negotiation are bad, you will want to work hard at reaching a negotiated settlement. On the other hand, if you have several viable alternatives to negotiation, you might be a tougher negotiator. You will be in a particularly

---

 BATNA

BATNA is an acronym for "best alternative to a negotiated agreement." The acronym was coined in the early 1980s in the book *Getting to Yes: Negotiating Agreement Without Giving In.* (For more information, see "The World at Your Fingertips" at the end of this chapter.) The term BATNA has since become widely used by negotiators and experts in the field.

---

strong position if you know that the other party has no good alternatives to negotiation.

Determining your BATNA requires a hard, rational look at your situation. One of the biggest mistakes people make is thinking that it will be easy to pursue alternatives to negotiation; they overestimate their BATNA. But BATNAs should not be based on wishful thinking about the best possible scenario if you walk away from the negotiating table. Rather, they should be based on the best *available* option you have if you are not able to work out an agreement.

To illustrate the importance of accurately assessing your BATNA, let's look at an example. Ron was a firefighter with a suburban fire department. When the department fired him after he fainted at work due to diabetes, Ron decided to sue the fire department for disability discrimination under the Americans With Disabilities Act. He asks for $2.5 million in damages. Ron and his lawyer discuss his situation with the fire department's lawyers, and the department offers Ron $50,000 and a pension based on his pay grade at the time he was fired. Ron believes he is better off going to court, because he thinks he has at least a 50 percent chance of winning the case. As a result, he values his BATNA at $1.25 million, which is the amount of damages for which he is suing ($2.5 million) times his likelihood of recovering that amount in court (50 percent, or 0.5).

Luckily, Ron's lawyer explains to Ron that $1.25 million is a significant overestimation of his BATNA. Specifically, he explains that disability suits against fire departments are very hard to win, because juries generally feel that firefighters should not be disabled. Winning in court is therefore far from certain. And even if Ron did win in court, prior jury awards suggest that it is unlikely he would get more than $25,000. In addition, going to court might risk Ron's pension. It would also require Ron to pay court costs and attorney's fees, which would further reduce the value of any damage award that he received at trial. After his attorney explains Ron's actual BATNA, Ron accepts the fire department's settlement offer.

Ron's story illustrates the importance of being realistic about your BATNA. If Ron had made a decision based on an assumed BATNA of $1.25 million, he may have been extremely disappointed with the outcome of his case in court.

It is also important to realize that BATNAs are not fixed. In fact, you should do everything you can to improve your BATNA before and even during a negotiation. A simple example will help to illustrate this principle. Imagine that you have been looking for a job for quite a while. Suppose you receive only one offer, from the music company Kathryn's Records. How strong is your negotiating position when it comes time to discuss your salary? The answer is, probably not very good. If you only have one job offer and you can't reach agreement on your salary, your BATNA is to keep looking and hope you find something else. (Your negotiating position will be particularly weak if Kathryn's Records knows this.) Now imagine you receive an offer from Johnny's Music as well as Kathryn's Records. Your negotiating position is suddenly much stronger, because any offer you receive from one company can be used as leverage against the other. Thus, whatever the value of the offer from Johnny's Music, you can ask Kathryn's Records to beat it. When the issue on the table is a salary with Kathryn's, your BATNA is a salary at Johnny's. In this situation, the more job offers you can get, the stronger your negotiating position will be.

This example illustrates an important principle: Improving your BATNA will improve your negotiating position. Your BATNA is your power in a negotiation; the better your BATNA, the more leverage you will have when negotiating.

Determine Your Target

Before you enter into a negotiation, make a detailed list of all the specific outcomes you want to achieve. Aim high, and ask yourself what conditions would leave you satisfied with the outcome. For example, if your position going into a salary negotiation is "I want a raise," your target might be a salary increase of 10 percent. To determine your target, you should create a statement of practical goals, such as a dollar figure or

▶ **DYNAMIC BATNAS**

Remember: Your BATNA is not fixed. You should be working to improve it by continuing to explore your alternatives to negotiation until the moment your dispute is resolved. And keep in mind that the other party's BATNA is not fixed, either.

a list of specific responses from the other party that will satisfy your interests.

Determining your target is the key to attaining satisfaction with a negotiation. There are three potential pitfalls to avoid: not setting a target, setting a target too low, and setting a target too high.

Consider what can happen if you don't set a target. Take Brad, who doesn't conduct any research before he negotiates and doesn't set any kind of target. Instead, he plans to reject any offer made by the other side and ask for more money—after all, he figures, if the other side is making the offer, it can't be a good deal. Brad doesn't know what he wants; he just knows that he doesn't want anything the other side is willing to offer. This is a phenomenon that researchers refer to as **reactive devaluation**. Reactive devaluation occurs when one party responds negatively to an offer simply because it was made by another party.

Suppose that Brad has a brother, Ringo. A few months ago, Brad and Ringo got into an argument over the estate left by their mother, Rosella, when she passed away. Ringo inventoried all of the property after Rosella's death, creating a list of things he wanted and a list of things he thought Brad would want. Ringo's list was very fair, and took into account the significance of certain items to each brother. In fact, had Brad inventoried the estate himself, he probably would have suggested an almost identical division of the property. However, as soon as Ringo made a proposal for dividing the estate, Brad decided that there had to be something wrong with his offer. Ringo got angry because he couldn't understand why Brad was being so unreasonable, and the two brothers ended up in a messy lawsuit. The lesson here is that Brad should have known what he wanted before he negotiated; he should have set his own target. If Brad had been ready to evaluate his options objectively, instead of basing his reaction on the *person* making the offer, he could have avoided going to court.

Another common mistake occurs when a person sets a target, but sets it too low. Suppose that Brad's friend, Eddie, is selling an antique table he inherited from a relative. Eddie decides what he would be willing to accept for the table, adds $200, and advertises the table in the local newspaper for $2,500 (his target price).

On the day the paper comes out, Eddie receives a call first thing in the morning from a dealer, who comes over and buys the table immediately, paying in cash. Eddie is initially thrilled. But throughout the rest of the day, Eddie receives dozens of additional phone calls. One caller tells him the table may have been worth as much as $15,000. Eddie realizes that he underestimated his target, and regrets selling the table for such a low price.

Eddie's example illustrates a phenomenon known as the **winner's curse**. Eddie got exactly what he wanted: $2,500. But even though he "won" by receiving the amount for which he asked, he *felt* like he had "lost"—that is, he felt like he could have done better. What was Eddie's mistake? He didn't do any research. Eddie had a number of options for determining what the table was worth. He could have looked at an antique valuation guide, or checked eBay for the value of similar items, or shopped around at other antique shops. He also could have talked to friends to get a better idea of how to sell antiques. But Eddie didn't do any of these things. Instead, he simply decided what he thought the table was worth and sold it. The lesson? Only by researching the value of a particular item or outcome can you be sure that you aren't setting your target too low.

A third mistake people often make is setting their targets too high. Let's go back to Eddie, who is frustrated and embarrassed by the low target he set when he sold the antique table. He decides that, the next time he has to negotiate, he will set a high target and refuse to budge. Eddie is a graphic designer, and is looking for a job. He receives an offer from a company, Designs Incorporated, for which he is very interested in working. Because he was making a $40,000 annual salary at his previous job, Eddie decides that he will not accept an offer of less than $50,000. But when he asks for $50,000, Designs Incorporated counters with an offer of $45,000. Eddie refuses to budge, assuming that if he is tough enough, the company will give in to his demands. Unfortunately for Eddie, however, his tough negotiating style strikes Designs Incorporated as unreasonable, and the firm ends up hiring someone else.

A month later, Eddie's savings run out and he ends up having to take a job designing Sunday advertisement circulars for Joe's Mattress World at an annual salary of $35,000. Eddie's mistake? Once again, he failed to do his research, and as a result he set his target too high. If he had researched the issue, he would have realized that many design companies—like Designs Incorporated—never pay people with his level of experience more than $45,000 per year, but that within two years he could have been making more than $60,000.

Setting your target might involve nothing more than a simple self-assessment and determination of your BATNA, but often it will also involve research. Comparison shopping is one way to conduct such research. For example, if you are thinking about buying a car, you should shop around. Today, much research can be done on the Internet. If you plan to buy or sell something, check out the price of similar items on Internet auction sites.

Remember: Your target is where you realistically *hope* to end up. If a negotiation ends at or very near your target, you should feel that you have had a very successful negotiating experience.

Set Your Reservation Point

Once you have determined your BATNA and your target, you are ready to set your reservation point. Your **reservation point** is the point at which you are willing to walk away from a deal and move

( ) TALKING TO A LAWYER

Q. I am trying to prepare for an upcoming salary negotiation. How do I ensure that I don't appear nonassertive by asking for too little, or greedy by asking for too much?

A. If you can, find out what other people in your company—and employees at other companies—make for performing jobs identical or similar to yours. Don't be afraid to ask for much more than you think you are likely to get; since you will almost never get more than you ask for, you may as well aim high. After all, unless you think that you might be fired (e.g., because of a recent bad evaluation or other nasty incident at work), what is the worst that can result from asking for too much? All your employer can do is say "no." And if your employer does reject your offer, then ask him or her to make an offer that he or she deems fair and reasonable. Then you'll have a high (your requested amount) and a low (your employer's offer), and you should be able to negotiate a raise somewhere in between.

—Answer by Judge Robert Shenkin,
Court of Common Pleas of Chester County,
West Chester, Pennsylvania

on to your BATNA. Put another way, your reservation point is the lowest offer you will accept before walking away.

Let's look at an example. Ernesto wants to sell his stereo, and solicits bids on Internet sites such as Craigslist. He receives an offer of $1,200. (The cost of selling over the Internet, including shipping and other charges, is $100.) Ernesto later meets to negotiate the sale of his stereo to his friend, Jacob. It may be tempting to assume that Ernesto's reservation point will be $1,100—that is, the price offered by the potential Internet buyer minus the cost of selling over the Internet. But this is not actually the case. The reason is that selling to Jacob presents certain advantages—for example, Ernesto would get his money right away, and he wouldn't incur the hassle of shipping. Thus, when negotiating with Jacob, Ernesto's reservation point should reflect these considerations. Ernesto sets his reservation point at $1,050. This means that any offer from Jacob lower than $1,050 will be unacceptable. Should Jacob offer less than $1,050, Ernesto can simply sell to the bidder from Craigslist for $1,200.

In this example, Ernesto uses his BATNA to help him determine his reservation point. Obviously, if Ernesto's BATNA was better—say, an offer of $2,000 from a buyer on eBay—then his reservation point would be higher. If Ernesto's BATNA was worse—for example, if he didn't have an online buyer and his next best alternative to selling to Jacob was to wait for another buyer—then he would set his reservation point lower.

Reservation points may also reflect emotional factors. For example, let's say that Eric and Georgia are getting divorced because Georgia had an affair with another partner at her law firm. Eric raised their three children while Georgia financially supported the family; his target is 50 percent of the couple's assets. Eric's BATNA is to go to court. If he does, he will almost certainly be able to secure a judgment entitling him to 50 percent of the marital estate. However, Eric really doesn't want to go to court. Going to court would mean testifying about his discovery of the affair, which he dreads. In this situation, Eric might decide that it would be worth 10 percent of the marital estate to avoid going to court. Therefore, Eric would set his reservation point in the negotiation at 40 percent of the marital estate.

Be careful not to confuse your target with your reservation point; they should not be the same. Your target is an outcome that you realistically hope to achieve, while your reservation point should be the worst deal that you will accept before walking away from the negotiation.

Evaluating the Other Party

After you have completed a self-assessment and formed a solid idea of what you want, why you want it, and what you'll settle for, you should evaluate your opponent. There are several factors to consider.

Who Are the Other Parties?

If you are involved in a dispute, it is very important to think about the identities of the other parties. In a dispute that seems to involve only one other person, consider whether a spouse, boss, relative, or other third party could be influencing the situation.

To help illustrate this principle, let's look at an example involving a dispute between neighbors. Seema plans to install a pool in her backyard. Seema's neighbor, Joy, threatens to sue her on the grounds that the pool construction will violate a town ordinance. Seema and Joy agree to sit down and discuss the matter to see if they can reach an agreement that will satisfy both of their interests. What Seema doesn't know, however, is that Joy doesn't really care about the pool. Rather, it is Joy's mother, Jennifer, who doesn't want it to be installed. Jennifer is worried that Seema's children will constantly play in the pool with friends and make a racket, which will disturb her peaceful gardening. When Seema meets to negotiate with Joy, she won't get very far unless she figures out who really has the problem with the pool, and why.

In addition to identifying the opposing parties, make sure that the person with whom you are negotiating has the authority to settle the dispute. For example, negotiating a raise with your supervisor will not get you very far if your supervisor does not have authority to give you a raise. Negotiating with the wrong person may be frustrating and futile.

What Are the Interests of the Other Party?

It is also important to think about the other party's interests. For instance, in the example involving the pool, Joy's main interest is in not hearing any complaints from her mother. She thinks that, in order to satisfy her interests, her mother must be able to continue gardening in the backyard undisturbed. Seema needs to recognize this interest in order to arrive at a mutually agreeable settlement. To accomplish this goal, Seema will likely have to spend a lot of time asking questions. Once Seema understands Joy's interests, she can decide how best to satisfy the interests of

▶ HOW TO HANDLE DIFFICULT QUESTIONS

Most people who are involved in a conflict believe that they are in the right. (If they didn't, there probably wouldn't be a conflict!) Great negotiators see the issues from all angles. To be a great negotiator, you must always be prepared to examine a conflict from the other party's point of view. This will help you anticipate and plan for difficult questions and issues. Remember, very few conflicts are totally one-sided.

Let's take an example. Cody and Monica are joint owners of a construction business. After a couple years of working together, they decide they would be better off working alone, so they end the business partnership. One of the main assets of the partnership is the tools that Cody and Monica have bought for the business. Cody wants to keep the tools, because he has another job lined up for which he can use them, and he doesn't have time to order new tools before the job starts. Monica is fine with letting Cody keep the tools, but she wants to be reimbursed for the cost of replacement tools. She calculates that replacing all the tools with brand-new models will cost $12,000.

When the pair meets to negotiate, Cody should be sure to ask Monica why she is basing her estimate of replacement cost on the price of new tools, when Cody will be left with used tools. Monica, in turn, should be prepared to answer this question. She could point out that finding new tools is easier than finding used tools, and that she wants to replace the tools quickly so she can accept more work. Cody, she could point out, will enjoy the benefit of having tools immediately. If Cody isn't amenable to this line of reasoning, she could suggest that they split the old tools, and each buy some new tools. But whatever solution they ultimately devise, the important point is that Monica must anticipate Cody's question and have a rational response prepared in advance.

both parties. For instance, she might determine that a fence would solve the problem, but she might want to ask Joy to pay for half of its construction cost.

What Is the Other Party's BATNA?

In a dispute, the other party's BATNA affects the settlement you will be willing to accept. If you know the other side's BATNA, you will know how much leverage over you that party enjoys, and the strength of their negotiating position.

Asking probing questions can be useful in determining the other party's BATNA. Sometimes the other side will be very tight-lipped, and will refuse to reveal any information about their alternatives to settlement. In these cases, independent research can be very useful. The Internet, friends, family, coworkers, attorneys, and the library are all potential sources of information that can help you determine another party's BATNA.

Identify Opportunities for a Win-Win Outcome

One of the most powerful things that negotiators can do is recognize or create opportunities for mutual gain. This means creating solutions that benefit both parties.

A real-life example can help illustrate this point. In 2003, a band called "The Postal Service" released an album on an independent label out of Seattle. The album became incredibly popular, receiving a great deal of radio play and publicity. Before long, the U.S. Postal Service (USPS) sued the band. It wanted the band to stop calling itself "The Postal Service," because that name is a trademark owned by the USPS.

After a thorough examination of the problem, however, the parties reached a negotiated agreement that was very creative. The band had chosen the name for a reason: its musicians had created an album despite living in different cities, and despite never actually recording together, by mailing recordings back and forth via the USPS. The USPS realized that this was an interesting story. Thus, instead of forcing the band to stop using its name, it asked the band to allow the use of its songs in USPS advertisements. Additionally, the band agreed to participate in commercials highlighting how it had made use of USPS services in order to make its album. In addition, the USPS began selling the album through its website.

In this situation, it would have been relatively easy for the USPS to stop the band from using its trademarked name. Luckily, however, both sides realized that they could benefit more from cooperating than from fighting.

This type of creative problem solving is where the magic really happens in negotiation. By looking at a situation from different angles and cooperating to achieve goals that will benefit both sides, parties can greatly ease the resolution of conflict. However, there's only one way to come up with solutions like this—and that's to prepare, prepare, prepare.

WHERE SHOULD NEGOTIATIONS TAKE PLACE?

According to many experts, negotiations should take place in a neutral location so that neither party has the advantage of bargaining on his or her home turf. An example of a neutral location is a local coffee shop or, for more sensitive matters, a conference room in a local library. Many mediation centers offer parties the option to rent rooms for negotiations. There is nothing magic about a neutral location, but it is important to be comfortable in the location where you will negotiate. Therefore, if you think that a neutral space will help you, ask for one. Make it clear that you will be more able to focus on problem solving in a neutral location; it will be difficult for the other side to argue with you.

THE NEGOTIATION PROCESS

Starting a negotiation can be very difficult. Instead of making an offer or a demand right off the bat, consider simply reviewing the situation with the other party. Go over the facts. Deter-

( ) TALKING TO A LAWYER

Q. When I'm making purchases, I hate negotiating. It makes me uncomfortable to ask for things like "free installation" or "future discounts," because I feel as though I'm asking for special treatment. Many of my friends and coworkers feel the same way. Are there ways to overcome negotiation aversion?

A. Yes. The best strategy is to remember that you're not really asking for "special" treatment. After all, you probably won't get anything that anyone else couldn't get if they were to ask. Why should you get less? If you ask for something, the other side can always just say "no." Another strategy is to try depersonalizing your request; instead of "Can I have a discount?" or "Can I have free installation?" try "Do you offer any discounts?" or "Do you offer free installation?" You can ask and still be nice. And if you do get more, congratulations! You're worth it.

—Answer by Judge Robert Shenkin,
Court of Common Pleas of Chester County,
West Chester, Pennsylvania

mine whether the other party sees the facts in the same way you do. Often, the source of a disagreement is one party's misunderstanding of the situation. Try to get the other party to agree that your common purpose is to reach a mutually acceptable agreement.

One of the first things to decide is whether you will make the first offer or wait for the other side to do so. Making the first offer is called **anchoring**, because a reasonable first offer "anchors" negotiations to a range of possible outcomes. Many people prefer to wait until the other side has made an offer; they are afraid that if they make the first offer, it will be lower than the other party's first offer would have been. But if you have done your homework, researched your subject, and set a target, you

▶ REDUCING POWER DIFFERENTIALS

If the other party seems more powerful than you, it is important to determine the reason for the imbalance. Is it because the other side has a lawyer present? If so, you could delay negotiations until you have an attorney, or state that you will only negotiate without a lawyer present if the other side is also unrepresented. Do you feel disadvantaged because the other side has brought four people to the negotiations, and you are by yourself? In that case, ask to call a friend who can help you out. Are you negotiating in a setting that is more comfortable for the other side? If so, ask for the negotiation to be moved to a neutral place. Remember, preparing well for the negotiation may reduce any such power differentials before negotiations begin.

---

should not be afraid to make the first offer. If you're the buyer, be sure to make an offer lower than your target so you will have room to negotiate. If you're selling something, be sure to make your first offer higher than the amount for which you actually want to sell—again, to leave yourself room to negotiate. However, do not start so high or low as to offend or insult the other side. You should anchor the negotiation at a reasonable point, which you can rationally justify. Research shows that the person who anchors the negotiation is more likely to perceive the outcome as satisfactory.

After you have made an offer, it is almost always best to wait for the other side to respond with an offer of its own (a **counteroffer**). Thus, if you offer $1,000 for a used car, and the seller rejects your offer but won't provide an amount for which he or she is willing to sell, you probably don't want to increase your offer until the seller has made an offer of his own. (This would be what's known as **bidding against yourself**.) If the other party refuses to make a counteroffer on the grounds that your offer is too unreasonable even to discuss, ask the other party if it really wants to reach agreement. If the other party won't make a counteroffer—particularly if you have increased your own offer at least once—it probably is not negotiating in good faith, and you should break off negotiations unless your BATNA is really terrible.

Remember: Negotiating is a process. As the negotiation progresses, expect some discussion and some give-and-take; the other party will expect the same thing. There may be several offers and counteroffers, but throughout the negotiation, keep your target firmly in mind.

DEALING WITH A DIFFICULT NEGOTIATOR

What if you prepare well for a negotiation, but are faced with a negotiator who just doesn't want to cooperate? Unfortunately, some people think that being rude or acting like a bully will get them what they want in a negotiation. This section will explain how to deal with this problem.

The first thing to remember is that you don't want to let things get personal. When someone is being rude or trying to bully you, it can be tempting to attack right back. However, this approach is generally unproductive in a negotiation. This does not mean that you should let anyone walk all over you. On the contrary, when dealing with a difficult negotiator you should be as assertive as possible—but you should be tough only in regards to the terms you are negotiating, not on a personal level in regards to the negotiator.

If you're faced with a tough negotiator, keep in mind the following tips:

1. **Try to ignore the behavior.** Like small children, some negotiators only engage in rude, unproductive behavior because it gets a rise out of the other party. If they don't get a reaction, they may cease the behavior. If ignoring the unacceptable behavior doesn't work, try responding to it directly. Sometimes simply calling attention to inappropriate actions (e.g., "There's no need to yell" or "I feel as though a threat is implied here; I hope that's not what you intend") can put a stop to bad behavior, or at least improve it.

2. **Focus on interests—yours and theirs.** Remind the other party that you are both there to reach a solution—not to continue arguing. Point out what the other side has to gain by reaching a settlement, such as avoiding the hassle of court, and that its interests likely will not be met if you are forced to end the negotiation.

3. **Suggest a break.** Sometimes people simply need some time to calm down. If things seem tense, try suggesting a break ("It seems like things are getting a little heated in here. Why don't we take a fifteen-minute break, or come back tomorrow and see if we can focus on the issues?").

4. **Consider mediation.** If you reach an impasse and simply can't seem to reason with the other party, a mediator may be able to help. Mediators are trained negotiation facilitators; often they can help parties reach an agreement even when agreement seems impossible.

5. **Walk away.** If a negotiation simply isn't working, don't be afraid to walk away. However, don't threaten to leave unless you are really ready to do so, and make sure you understand your BATNA and the consequences of abandoning the negotiation. Empty threats will undermine your credibility at the negotiating table, and are a dangerous negotiating tactic that should rarely—if ever—be used.

ENFORCING A NEGOTIATED AGREEMENT

Even if you reach a mutually satisfactory agreement through negotiation, you aren't done yet. Once you reach agreement, it is important to document the agreement and come up with a means of enforcing it. If the subject matter is sufficiently important, the parties should hire a lawyer to formalize the agreement in a binding contract. However, in some cases it may be acceptable for the parties simply to write out their understanding of what they have agreed. Usually, if a mutually beneficial agreement has been reached, there is mutual incentive for the parties to abide by the agreement, and enforcement won't be an issue.

▶ **PREPARING FOR A NEGOTIATION**

1. Determine your interests. What do you want from the negotiation, and, more importantly, why do you want it?

2. Determine your best alternative to a negotiated agreement (BATNA). That is, if you can't reach an agreement with the other party, what is your next best option? The better your BATNA, the better your bargaining position.

3. Determine your target—that is, the specific outcomes you want to achieve in the negotiation. You may need to do some research to work out a realistic target.

4. Set your reservation point—that is, your bottom line. Generally, this should be slightly better than your BATNA.

5. Analyze the other party. What do they care about? What are their needs and interests? What is their BATNA? What are you willing to give them? What are the hard questions with which they will confront you?

Keep in mind that aligning the parties' incentives will help bring the negotiated agreement to fruition. Putting the agreement into writing will give both parties the right to take each other to court if the agreement is not carried out. A lawyer can help you create appropriate wording for the agreement.

THE WORLD AT YOUR FINGERTIPS

- *Getting to Yes: Negotiating Agreement Without Giving In* by Bruce Patton, Roger Fisher, and William Ury (2nd edition, Penguin Books, 1991) is an excellent introduction to negotiating all kinds of disputes. This is the seminal book on interest-based negotiation.

- *The Mind and Heart of the Negotiator* by Leigh Thompson (3rd edition, Prentice Hall, 2005) explores concepts of negotiation in an easy-to-follow format.

ⓘ COLLABORATIVE LAW

Collaborative law is a relatively new area of law in which parties seek to work with lawyers to resolve disputes without contested court hearings. Under principles of collaborative law, the parties hire attorneys on the understanding that those attorneys can only be used to help negotiate a settlement to the dispute. If the case is not resolved, then the parties must hire new lawyers to handle a trial.

The parties and their attorneys sign a contract agreeing to work toward a settlement without going to court or threatening to go to court. This contract, known as a **participation agreement**, also stipulates that all proceedings will be confidential. In collaborative arrangements, both sides are expected to act openly and in good faith. A free and open exchange of relevant information is key to making the process work. Your lawyer will still advocate for you, but all parties have the same goal in mind: a fair and equitable settlement.

Collaborative law is primarily used in family law, but is also used to resolve disputes involving employment law, business law, wills and estates, medical law, and personal injury. Collaborative law provides a structure that may result in an efficient settlement of the parties' disputes—*if* the parties are ready to negotiate in good faith.

- The Association for Conflict Resolution has an extensive website that includes articles and background information about how to use negotiations to resolve conflicts effectively. You can access these resources at *www.acrnet.org*.
- You can learn about cutting-edge research, and find an assortment of articles on negotiation and conflict resolution, at the online clearinghouse of the Program on Negotiation at Harvard Law School, at *www.pon.org/catalog/index.php*.
- For more information about collaborative law, visit the Collaborative Law Center at *www.collaborativelaw.com*.

REMEMBER THIS

- Anyone can learn to negotiate effectively.
- Almost anything can be negotiated.
- Preparation is the key to a successful negotiation.
- The better you understand your interests and those of the other party, the more effectively you will be able to craft a solution that will satisfy both sides.
- Your BATNA is your leverage over the other party. Do everything you can to improve your BATNA before you start negotiating. Make every effort to improve your BATNA as you continue negotiating.
- Take some time to do some research and set a realistic target.
- Think about the position, interests, BATNA, and target of the other party. An accurate assessment of the other side will help you anticipate tough questions, and will put you in a stronger position going into the negotiation.

CHAPTER 3

Mediation

Three Heads are Better Than Two

Six-year-old twins Juan and Rose are fighting about who should have access to their tree house. They ask their mother to decide, and she helps them work out a schedule for sharing it.

Down the street, Mr. and Mrs. Saunders are in the process of getting a divorce. They hire a mediator to help them reach consensus on how to divide their property.

At DiBase Corporation, negotiations regarding a possible merger with another company have stalled. The managing director asks a mediator to assist in helping move negotiations forward.

At an international level, the United States is involved in a trade dispute about its right to sell genetically modified food in Europe. Representatives of the U.S. and the European Union meet with a mediator to see if they can resolve the problem.

Mediation is a voluntary, confidential process for resolving disputes—a process in which a neutral third party, the **mediator**, helps parties reach a resolution. Mediation affords the parties to a dispute a great deal of control. The role of the third party is confined to assisting with the negotiations; mediators do not take sides, and do not make binding decisions.

Mediation is used by families, businesses, and organizations, and as a diplomatic tool for resolving international conflicts. No case is too large or small for mediation. For example, if Tina sues her landlord for an unreturned security deposit in the amount of $700, a court might refer her case to mediation. On the other end of the spectrum, if Pollution, Inc. is sued for contaminating the rivers of Smallville and causing birth defects in babies, the company could also settle the case through mediation—even with millions of dollars at stake.

▶ IS YOUR CASE APPROPRIATE FOR MEDIATION?

Whether a dispute is appropriate for mediation depends on a number of factors relating to the interests of the parties involved in the dispute. Your dispute may be suitable for mediation if:

- You have an ongoing relationship with the other person
- You don't feel unduly pressured, coerced, or under duress from the other party to do something you don't want to do
- You feel that you can negotiate and speak in your own best interest
- You are emotionally invested in the issues at stake
- The case involves more than money
- You want or need a quicker, more expedient outcome than court would allow
- There are no lawyers involved (although attorneys can be involved if you want)
- You think it would help the situation if you could speak directly to the other side
- There are multiple people involved in the dispute

Your case is probably not appropriate for mediation if:

- There is ongoing abuse of one party by another
- There is a history of domestic violence between the parties
- The other party is not trustworthy or negotiating in good faith
- The issue is not negotiable
- You want to set a precedent in court

Mediation is a common tool in a wide variety of disputes, including:

- Workplace disputes relating to:
  - Discrimination (on the basis of age, gender, disability, religion, race, or national origin)
  - Complaints regarding management
  - Wrongful termination
  - Harassment
  - Strife between coworkers
- Family disputes relating to:
  - Wills and estates
  - Divorce
  - Child custody and visitation arrangements
  - Family businesses
  - Medical decisions
  - Parent-child issues
  - Adult guardianship issues
  - End-of-life issues
- Public disputes relating to:
  - Land use
  - The environment
  - Community projects
  - School management
- General disputes relating to:
  - Business agreements
  - Construction, landscaping, and home maintenance contracts
  - Landlord-tenant issues

As the list above makes clear, mediation can be used to resolve almost any type of dispute in which people don't see eye to eye. However, this does not mean that every dispute must be mediated. A judge may certainly order parties in a case to participate in mediation, but neither the judge nor the mediator can force you to reach an agreement. Mediation is a voluntary process, meaning *you* choose whether or not to come to an agreement through mediation.

This chapter will describe the role of the mediator, and outline

(i) NOTHING NEW UNDER THE SUN

While it may seem as though mediation is something relatively recent and even "trendy," there is nothing new about the age-old practice of trying to resolve a legal problem through assisted negotiation. China's earliest recorded and oral history tells us that mediation was used to resolve disputes thousands of years ago. Ancient Chinese mediators were heads of families and clans. They discouraged formal legal procedures because of the detrimental effect they had on families and communities, and instead encouraged peaceful resolutions that involved apologies and compromise.

the basic steps that take place in most mediations, large or small. We will go on to look at some of the advantages and disadvantages of mediation in particular circumstances, to give you a better idea of whether mediation is a useful tool to help you resolve your dispute.

( ) TALKING TO A LAWYER

Q. It seems to me that mediation circumvents the judicial system to a troubling degree. After all, mediation causes more and more people to resolve disputes in private, behind closed doors, when such disputes should be a matter of public discussion. Is this a matter for concern?

A. There are certainly cases in which legal precedent is both necessary and important. However, mediation is about self-determination for the parties. Therefore, it should be up to the parties to determine how they want their dispute to proceed, and how they want it to be resolved. In cases where legal precedent is important for society as a whole, litigating parties should resolve their dispute through the court system.

—Answer by Cookie Levitz, mediator,
Chicago, Illinois

THE MEDIATOR

Mediators come from all walks of life. Anyone who enjoys creative problem solving and is comfortable with conflict can become a mediator. Mediators come from all professions—they might be social workers, therapists, clergy, teachers, human resources personnel, managers, or consultants—and many are attorneys. Retired judges also sometimes serve as mediators.

The mediator is neutral and impartial—he or she has no vested interest in the outcome of the case, and has no conflict of interest with the mediation participants.

Which Type of Mediator is Right for You?

There are three general approaches to mediation: facilitative, evaluative, and transformative. Very few mediators practice one type of mediation exclusively; most mediators use techniques from different models to help parties achieve their goals. The mediator may even begin a mediation playing a facilitative role, and switch to an evaluative role if the parties do not reach agreement.

Facilitative Mediation

A **facilitative mediator** facilitates discussion and negotiations between the parties. The parties control the process and agenda—they make decisions about how each side should present its case, when to negotiate together, and when each side should meet separately with the mediator. The mediator does not evaluate the strength of each side's case, or advocate for any particular outcome. Rather, the mediator's role is to help the parties explore their mutual interests, and to ask questions to ensure that the parties understand their own needs and options. A facilitative mediator neither "settles" a case nor offers ideas or proposals. Facilitative mediation is common in community-based mediation programs.

Evaluative Mediation

An **evaluative mediator** controls the mediation process to a much greater extent than a facilitative mediator, and may even influence its outcome by evaluating the case. The prototype of an evaluative mediator is a retired judge, or a lawyer with substantive legal expertise in the subject of the mediation. Many mediators will begin mediating in a facilitative role, and then switch to an evaluative approach if facilitation does not work. In evaluative mediation, parties are influenced by and rely on the mediator's assessment of the case. An evaluative mediator will try to "settle" the case, and may offer his or her own proposals and suggestions for how to end the dispute.

Transformative Mediation

A **transformative mediator** looks to the parties to control the mediation process as well as the outcome, and seeks out opportunities for the parties' empowerment and mutual recognition. He or she emphasizes the ability of the parties to make better decisions for themselves, and helps them to consider each other's perspectives and experiences. When possible, the transformative mediator is concerned with creating empathy and acknowledgment between the parties. As a result, the transformative model of mediation is devoid of any pressure on the parties to come to an agreement. This type of mediation is relatively new, but has been employed by some large organizations including the United States Postal Service.

Mediator Training

Most mediators who work in courts and community organizations have completed a certification process of some sort. Mediation training can include several days of classes on mediation theory, ethics, and skill building, which are often taught through role-play so that the mediator can practice mediation skills before using them in real disputes. Mediation training programs vary in length, but generally entail about forty hours of training

NO NATIONAL STANDARDS

Currently there are no national training standards for mediators, nor is there a standard certification process. In addition, there is often no system of state certification. This means that, for mediators, there is no equivalent to the CPA exam taken by accountants, or the bar exam taken by lawyers. However, as mediation and other forms of alternative dispute resolution increase in popularity in the United States, the call for national certification is growing. Some states such as Illinois have adopted the Uniform Mediation Act, which regulates mediator privilege and the confidentiality of mediations. In addition, many individual associations that provide mediators, such as the Judicial Arbitration Mediation Services (JAMS), have established their own internal certification requirements.

and instruction. Various organizations and community centers offer mediator training and certify both lawyers and nonlawyers as mediators. ("The World at Your Fingertips" section at the end of this chapter includes more information about where to pursue mediation training and certification.)

How To Choose a Mediator

Once you have chosen mediation as the means for resolving your dispute, you will need to select a mediator. The mediator you choose will control the mediation process. Because of this, it is important to choose someone who is qualified, and with whom you are comfortable working. In particular, you should choose a mediator whom you believe will be fair and impartial.

When selecting a mediator, some factors to consider include:

• **Experience.** What types of cases has the mediator handled? Does he or she have expertise in a particular field?

• **Reputation.** Does the mediator have a reputation for professionalism and fairness?

(i) RESTORATIVE JUSTICE

Imagine a shopkeeper runs a comic book store in a small town. The shopkeeper often lets adolescents thumb through comics, and talks with them about their favorite heroes or inkers. One night, a teenager breaks into the store, stealing money and expensive comics. He is caught, sent to juvenile detention for four months and put on probation for a year. After the incident the owner installs an expensive alarm. He regards his teenage clientele with suspicion. Other stores in the neighborhood that cater to the same age group begin to limit the number of teenagers in their stores. Teens start to feel angry and stereotyped. The entire community suffers.

Restorative justice seeks to heal the injury done to the victim, the community, and the offender. There are four key elements to restorative justice:

1. *Encounters.* Victims are given the chance to talk with offenders and community members about the crime and the effects it had.

2. *Amends.* Offenders are given the chance to mend the problems they created.

3. *Reintegration.* All involved deal with the mental and emotional traumas of the crime.

4. *Inclusion.* People who have been affected by a particular crime are given the chance to take part in its resolution.

There are many different types of restorative justice programs. In Victim-Offender Mediation (VOM), the victims have the chance to tell the offender how they were affected by his or her crimes. The offender can apologize. A neutral third party trained in facilitating dialogue runs the sessions. Restorative justice includes elements of both mediation and arbitration.

Many youth courts are also operated along restorative justice principles. In youth courts, young offenders who have admitted guilt are sentenced by a jury of their peers. The sentences are designed to heal the injury done to the victim and the community. There are more than 1,000 youth courts across the United States, in 49 states.

- **Accreditation.** Is the mediator certified through a reputable training program? Is he or she affiliated with a reputable organization?
- **Style of mediation.** Do you want the mediator to make suggestions and evaluate your options, or would you prefer a mediator who simply facilitates dialogue?

If you do not want to choose a mediator yourself, or if the parties cannot agree on a mediator, you can turn the selection process over to a nonprofit or for-profit organization. Some organizations that facilitate mediation will send both sides a list of mediators who are qualified in the relevant area, and will include information about the mediators' backgrounds. If the parties cannot agree on a mediator, the facilitator will appoint one. Provider organizations work to make sure that their mediators are impartial and have no conflicts of interest in the cases to which they are assigned. In addition to helping with the selection process, many organizations offer help in administering mediations.

HOW DOES A DISPUTE GET TO MEDIATION?

A dispute can get to mediation in several different ways. You and the other party to your dispute may agree to a mediation. Or your lawyer, if you have one, may suggest that you mediate your dispute in order to save time and money. Sometimes judges will order or suggest mediation. Or a contract may specify that any disputes under that contract must be mediated.

A dispute may be ripe for mediation while an existing lawsuit is pending; as the costs of preparing for litigation take their toll, financially and otherwise, parties may become more willing to mediate. Mediators often say that parties have nothing to lose in mediation; they can only gain. In other words, mediation may help you settle a lawsuit, and even if the mediation is unsuccessful, you will be no worse off for having tried. Even a failed mediation can provide insight into the other side's case, and you

will know more about what will be required to settle your dispute. In addition, disputes generally provide few formal opportunities for non-adversarial dialogue. But mediation allows
parties to communicate face-to-face, which can be extremely
productive in terms of breaking an impasse or kick-starting
negotiations.

Several state courts, such as those in California, Minnesota,
New York, and Florida, require mediation for certain types of
cases. Courts cannot force parties to settle cases, but they can
require parties to attend mediation with a court-appointed or
private mediator.

▶ WHEN IS A DISPUTE RIPE FOR MEDIATION?

Before entering into mediation, consider whether the following conditions are met:

- The people on both sides have the authority to settle the case
- Both sides are ready to negotiate in good faith
- You are ready to talk about the events that led to the dispute
- You have thought about your needs and interests
- You have a list of possible solutions to present to the other side
- You have a list of questions for the other side that will help you col-
  lect the information you need to make decisions
- You have researched the law relating to your dispute, so you have at
  least some idea about your alternatives if you do not resolve the
  matter in mediation
- You understand the process of mediation and know what to expect

THE MEDIATION PROCESS

While all mediations vary, most follow the same basic pattern. This section will provide an overview of the procedures generally involved.

The First Steps in Mediation

To provide the mediator with some context for your case, the first step in any mediation is to outline the nature of the dispute. If the case is small and there are no lawyers involved, and particularly if the mediation is at a community center or workplace, a case manager or secretary usually will consult with the parties and summarize the dispute for the mediator in a short paragraph.

Parties represented by lawyers generally submit a short summary of the case. This summary typically highlights their demands, provides support for their positions, and indicates the procedural status of the case, which is relevant if the parties are preparing for a trial. The mediator will review these statements to obtain background information prior to the mediation.

The Mediator's Opening Statement

At the outset of mediation, the mediator, the parties, and any support persons or attorneys accompanying the parties usually will be together in the same room. The mediator typically begins the mediation with an opening statement, in which he or she sets the agenda and defines his or her role as a neutral third party. The mediator will explain that he or she is not a judge, and thus will not be issuing a ruling of any kind, and that the process is confidential. He or she will also point out any circumstances in which the process will *not* be confidential, such as those involving threats of imminent harm. Often the mediator will check with the parties to ensure that they are the appropriate parties for the mediation (i.e., that they have authority to settle the dispute). The mediator will also confirm that he or she has no outside involvement with either party, and will state that he or she is impartial. He or she will also set ground rules regarding civility.

The Parties' Opening Statements and Dialogue

Each party has an opportunity to tell its story, either on its own or through an attorney. The person who initiated the mediation usually goes first. The mediator then invites the second party to give a brief statement. The mediator initiates dialogue between the parties by asking some questions about the dispute. At this stage of the proceedings, the mediator is gathering information, and the parties are exchanging information. The parties are free to discuss whatever topics they would like.

The opportunity to engage in constructive dialogue is perhaps one of the most significant benefits of mediation. In litigation, the parties talk to the judge or jury, often through lawyers, but rarely or never speak directly to each other. In mediation, the parties can and often do ask questions or make comments (e.g., "Why did you do that to me?" or "You could have talked to me first . . ."). This type of open, direct communication creates valuable opportunities for understanding and healing.

Caucusing

The mediator may then **caucus** with each party. This means that he or she may meet privately with each side to assess its needs and interests, identify common ground, explore settlement options, and "smoke out" hidden agendas. Often the mediator will ask the parties some "reality check" questions in private, to ensure that they understand the likely outcome of their actions. An evaluative mediator may also offer an assessment of the case in confidence. The mediator will keep confidential anything the parties don't want revealed to each other.

During this process, the mediator may shuttle back and forth between rooms while the parties remain separated. This is sometimes called **shuttle diplomacy**. The mediator can present various proposals at one time, or take the same proposal back and forth multiple times. If the parties can reach agreement during the shuttling, the mediator may call the parties and/or the lawyers back together to document the agreement.

Following the caucuses with individual parties, the mediator will reconvene a joint session in which both sides are present, and will guide the parties as they generate and evaluate settlement options. The mediator again may ask "reality check" questions to help the parties predict the consequences of various settlement options. When possible solutions emerge, the mediator may help the parties refine them by asking specific questions: Who will do what? When will it be done? Where and how will it be done? What will happen if things don't work out as expected? Will the parties return to mediation or proceed to trial?

The Agreement Stage

If the parties reach an agreement, the mediator may document in writing the substance of that agreement. Sometimes written agreements are signed by the parties, and sometimes not. When attorneys are involved, the mediator is more likely to list the decisions of the parties in a document called a **memorandum of understanding**. The attorneys will then translate the memorandum into legal language, add boilerplate (i.e., standard) terms, and draft a formal contract or court submission that will become a legally binding document.

If a court-appointed mediator brokers an agreement between parties involved in a lawsuit, the parties generally agree to drop the suit. Most judges will order that a lawsuit be dropped **without prejudice**, meaning that if one party does not comply with the agreement reached in mediation, the other party can resume the lawsuit.

If no agreement is reached, the mediator will facilitate a discussion between the parties about their options. Sometimes when the parties consider their alternatives to reaching a mediated agreement, they begin to loosen up and make some compromises. Even if the parties cannot agree, they haven't lost much by mediating, and have usually gained knowledge about a case and some insight into what is motivating the other side.

Enforcement

Most mediation agreements are as enforceable as any other contract, meaning that one party can ask a court to enforce the agreement if the other party does not comply.

( ) TALKING TO A LAWYER

Q. *I was discriminated against at work, and my employer encouraged me to try resolving the problem through mediation. They even paid for a mediator. But the human resources representative from my company knew more about the law than I did, and she kept saying I would lose in court. I believed her at the mediation, so I settled for an amount much smaller than I wanted. What can I do now?*

A. Probably nothing. If, as you say, you **settled**—meaning that you entered into an agreement, especially a written agreement, in which you agreed to accept a sum of money in return for releasing your employer from further liability—then you are probably bound by your agreement. Nonetheless, you should do now what you should have done before the mediation: consult a lawyer with knowledge and experience in employment law. It is possible that your settlement isn't binding on you, or that it could be set aside—that is, ignored as though it doesn't exist—for any number of legal reasons. Or you might still have legal remedies in spite of having agreed to settle. Or maybe you will learn that the human resources rep was right—that your legal case was weak, and that your settlement was a reasonable one. But even if this turns out to be the case, confirming it with a lawyer may give you some peace of mind.

—Answer by Judge Robert Shenkin,
Court of Common Pleas of Chester County,
West Chester, Pennsylvania

( ) TALKING TO A LAWYER

Q. *I slipped on some grapes in my local supermarket and injured my back. In mediation, the supermarket owner agreed to pay my medical bills plus $5,000. However, six months later the bills still haven't been paid, and I haven't seen a check. What can I do now?*

A. Send a copy of the written mediated settlement agreement to the supermarket owner, along with a letter explaining that you have not received payment. If that doesn't work, go to small-claims court (assuming the jurisdictional limit in your state is less than $5,000), bring a copy of the settlement agreement, and file a claim.

—Answer by Professor Joseph L. Daly,
Hamline University School of Law,
Saint Paul, Minnesota

THE PROS AND CONS OF MEDIATION

There are several advantages and disadvantages to mediation. As a result, it may be more suitable in some circumstances than others. This section will help you decide whether mediation might be right for you.

Saved Relationships

Unlike a court case in which one side wins and the other loses, mediation offers an opportunity for both parties to be satisfied with the outcome. Because of this, it is often possible for the parties to preserve a good relationship during and after mediation.

An example will help to illustrate this principle. Imagine that neighbors Luis and Steve get into an argument over a fallen tree. The tree, which originally stood on the dividing line between their properties, damaged Steve's house when it fell. Steve wants

Luis to pay for a portion of the repairs to his house, because the tree started out partly in Luis's yard. Things heat up, and Steve sues Luis for $5,000, which is half the amount that it will cost to fix the house.

If Steve and Luis end up in court, a judge will issue a decision. Steve will either receive $5,000, a lesser amount, or nothing. If Steve wins, Luis is likely to feel angry, bitter, and frustrated. If Luis wins, Steve will likely be angry, and will feel that the result was unfair. If the two could walk away from court and never see each other again, this might not be such a big deal. But they can't; Steve and Luis are neighbors and will have to continue living next to each other. Steve's children play with Luis's children, and they are both active members of their community. Any bitterness resulting from a court case is likely to have a negative effect on their interactions long after the judge issues a decision. Thus, even the "winner" of the lawsuit will probably end up being disappointed with the outcome.

In this example, mediation presents a good alternative for resolving the dispute. Mediation would give Steve and Luis the opportunity to devise a mutually agreeable solution with which both of them can be satisfied. If they are able to reach a compromise, their relationship after the dispute will be far more amicable than if they go to court and only one side "wins."

In any dispute, if the parties reach an agreement that satisfies them both, it will make their ongoing relations much more pleasant—whether they live next door to each other, work together, do business together, or see each other at family get-togethers. While few relationships can survive a court case that puts the participants at odds, mediation offers the opportunity to strengthen relationships by allowing the parties to explain their interests and devise mutually agreeable solutions.

Creative Problem Solving

Another advantage of mediation is that it gives people the opportunity to solve problems creatively. Courts generally can offer only a narrow range of solutions, usually in the form of either monetary awards or orders for a party to take some action or cease some behavior. (See chapter 6, "Court Procedures for Civil Cases," for more information on remedies available in court.) In mediation, however, a much broader range of solutions is possible.

For example, suppose a Home Depot is slated for construction in the community of Montrose. The Montrose residents are upset about the potential for increased traffic and a negative impact on some small businesses in the area, and go to court seeking an order to stop the construction. In a courtroom context, the judge could either halt construction or allow it to go forward. In mediation, however, the range of potential solutions is limited only by the creativity of the parties and the mediator involved. Thus, before construction moves forward, the parties could agree to a course of action that would satisfy them both—for example, conducting further research in Montrose and surrounding areas, or holding town hall meetings in order to discuss the proposed construction. Perhaps all parties would be happier with a new Home Depot accessible to Montrose residents, but in a less populated area. The store's ultimate success may hinge on the goodwill gained in mediation.

Let's return for a moment to Steve and Luis's neighborly dispute over the fallen tree. As we established earlier, if the parties go to court, either Steve or Luis will win and not have to pay for the damage; the other will lose and have to pay. Suppose now that Luis is a contractor. In mediation, Luis might agree to contribute his services if Steve buys the materials needed for the repairs. This type of creative solution is uniquely available in mediation, and wouldn't be possible if the case went to court. Sometimes the only remedy one party wants is an apology.

The creative-problem-solving aspect of mediation allows those involved to take control of the outcome in a way that is not possible in court. Mediation often leads to outcomes that are a better fit for the situation, which in turn means that the parties are more likely to comply with whatever agreement they reach.

Savings of Time and Money

Mediation is less expensive than going to court, a fact that accounts for much of its increasing appeal as a dispute resolution tool. There are many costs associated with going to court (see chapter 6, "Court Procedures for Civil Cases," for more information), perhaps the most significant of which is the cost of a lawyer. Most people underestimate the cost of hiring an attorney, primarily because they have no idea how long it will take an attorney to work on their case. Lawyers charge for their time, and what might seem to a client like a simple matter may actually involve complicated research and in-depth preparation. The time spent interviewing clients and witnesses also costs money. Preparing for even the simplest jury trial usually takes well over a hundred hours. And at a modest rate of, say, $150 dollars per hour, those hundred hours add up to a lot of legal fees. Some attorneys do work for a **contingency fee**, which means they are paid only if the client wins the case. Lawyers working under this kind of arrangement are paid a percentage—often 33 percent—of any award the client receives. Chapter 7 provides more information about the costs of working with a lawyer.

Parties choosing mediation can save money in lawyers' fees because the mediation process does not take as long as the trial process. There are fewer formalities in mediation, which means that preparation takes less time. And during mediation, both sides simply present their sides of the story and then try to work out a solution. This means that, even in situations where both sides have lawyers, it's much less expensive to mediate than to go to court.

Of course, the parties may need to pay a mediator. Many community centers offer free, sliding-scale, or low-cost mediation. The cost of a private mediator varies widely, from $50 to $2,000 per hour. A court-appointed mediator often works for free or at a nominal rate for the parties. Usually the parties agree to split the cost of the mediator. If an individual is involved in a lawsuit with a corporation, the corporation will sometimes pay for the mediation. This happens frequently in employment matters.

Having Your Day in Court

Sometimes people involved in a dispute simply want a "day in court" to air their grievances in a public forum. However, going to court is usually much less satisfying than people expect. Remember: In a lawsuit, the plaintiff and defendant only get to testify about things the judge thinks are relevant to the situation. The parties don't get to choose what they talk about. Instead, they answer narrowly tailored questions from their own attorney, and face tough questions from the other side's attorney. The opponent's questions are adversarial in nature, and usually are designed to focus on facts the party most wants to avoid.

Let's imagine that Anna sues Harry for selling her a used car that broke down after only two days. Anna is incredibly mad at Harry because now she can't get to work. Anna also can't take her mother, Sandra, to the hospital for her weekly appointments, and instead has to take Sandra on the bus, which takes two hours in each direction. Anna really wants to go to court so she can explain to the judge and Harry how difficult the car's breakdown has made her life. What Anna should know, however, is that the judge is unlikely to let her talk about all the things that have gone wrong since she bought the faulty car. Most likely, the judge will only want to hear factual details about when she bought the car, how much she paid, and whether there was an explicit warranty. If Anna goes to court hoping to tell her entire story, she is likely to be very disappointed.

Ultimately, Anna may be better off in mediation. Mediation is open-ended, which means there are no limits on what the parties can discuss. If Anna wants to spend time talking about the troubles she's had since the car broke down, she can do so.

Confidentiality

Unless a judge orders otherwise, everything that happens in court is public—the public can attend hearings and trials, and the court makes publicly available the decisions made by judges and juries. This transparency of the court process is important to our legal system. It means that the public can see how the system works, and feel confident that the system is fair, unbiased, and consistent.

Decisions made in court also have wide application. A decision will apply not only to the parties involved in a specific case, but also to other people in similar circumstances. For example, suppose a person is harassed at work. If that person goes to court, his or her story will be made public, and the employer may be prevented from harassing employees in the future. In the movie *North Country*, the main character, played by Charlize Theron, sues her employer on behalf of fellow female employees who have been sexually harassed. These women want a public forum in which to tell the story of what they have endured. They want their community to know what has happened—both to elicit outrage, and to prevent similar treatment of other employees in the future. If the heroine of *North Country* had decided to mediate the issue of harassment, the resolution of her case would have been confidential. It may not have changed the company's behavior, and would have had no effect on other employers. But when a case goes to court, the publicity generated—as with the real-life case that inspired the film—can motivate people elsewhere in the country to change their behavior. In this way, courts can sometimes be agents for social change.

While people in some situations want their stories to be made public, others want to keep their disputes behind closed doors. Consider Millhouse, a foreman at a construction site who had too many beers at a retirement luncheon for a coworker. After lunch, he went back to work and caused an accident in which another employee, Lisa, was injured. Millhouse is accused of negligence. In a situation like this, mediation would probably be in Millhouse's best interest. Because mediation is confidential, it will allow Millhouse to prevent anyone else from finding out that his drinking may have caused an accident. If Lisa simply wants to resolve her case and move on, she might also be satisfied with mediation. On the other hand, if her employer condones working while drunk and other accidents have occurred under similar circumstances, Lisa might decide to pursue a court case in order to make the issue public and prevent similar accidents from ever happening again.

Another point to consider is that a mediator will keep all facts learned through mediation confidential. He or she will not willingly testify or report on any discussions that occur during mediation. The mediator's notes are never shared with the parties, and are usually destroyed at the conclusion of the mediation. A court considers mediation a **settlement conference** (discussed further in chapter 6), and court rules prohibit statements made in settlement conferences from being used against the parties in a trial.

Keep in mind, however, that with respect to the confidentiality of mediation, certain exceptions may apply. For example, if a mediator learns that someone is at risk of imminent harm, he or she may breach the confidentiality of the mediation. Or if the mediator is an attorney and observes unethical conduct by another attorney, he or she might be required by law to report it to a state agency that regulates and disciplines attorneys. Exceptions to the principle of mediator confidentiality vary from state to state, depending on the statutes that apply.

Winning

One advantage of mediation is that it results in an agreement tailored to the parties' individual circumstances, rather than a one-size-fits-all ruling from the courts. The power of a mediated agreement derives from the fact that the parties base it on their own needs and interests, and are thus invested in it. Each party stands to gain from the agreement, and thus agrees to it.

For example, suppose a parent files a grievance claiming that her child's school district is failing to provide the child with mandated special-education services. The school district might refer the child, the parent, and the school officials to mediation in order to give the parties an opportunity to reach agreement. If they do reach an agreement, that agreement will reflect the fact that the problems at hand have been resolved at some level. The parties will agree in good faith to stick to the terms of the agree-

ⓘ THE PREROGATIVES AND POWERS OF JUDGES AND MEDIATORS

Mediators are concerned with:

- The needs and interests of the parties
- Problem solving
- Building relationships
- Finding creative solutions
- Creating opportunities for communication between the parties

Mediators don't have any legal authority and can't force parties to do anything. However, mediators have the power to make suggestions and proposals, which can be accepted or rejected by the parties.

Judges are concerned with:

- The law
- Precedent
- The facts of the situation
- Court procedure
- Determining the "truth"

A judge has the power to:

- Decide who wins and loses
- Issue orders compelling people to do certain things or refrain from certain actions
- Issue a decision that will be part of the public record
- Control and restrict what is discussed in the courtroom

ment, and usually will do so because the agreement reflects both of their interests. Moreover, both parties maintain the full legal right to initiate a hearing at any time.

Parties who feel a need to "win," and to hear a judge place blame on the other party, are unlikely to find satisfaction in mediation. For instance, suppose Joan and Steve take their son, Edgar, to the state fair. While there, Edgar rides a roller coaster and ends up flying from his seat because the cart is not adequately designed to contain a person of his small stature. Edgar is severely injured. He is now in a wheelchair, and may not walk again without a cane. In this case, it might be very important for Joan and Steve to hear a judge tell the roller coaster company that it was negligent. If they choose mediation to resolve their case, they will not get this satisfaction, even if the company issues a confidential apology. A mediator will not determine either party to be at fault. One party may admit fault to the other as part of a settlement, but a mediator will not tell either party that it is "wrong." If Steve and Joan want to hear someone in authority tell the roller coaster company that its negligence caused Edgar's injury, they will have to go to court.

THE WORLD AT YOUR FINGERTIPS

• More information about community-based mediation, including a list of community mediation centers nationwide, can be found on the website of the National Association for Community Mediation at *www.nafcm.org*.

• There are several resources you can use to find a mediator. The Mediate.com website, at *www.mediate.com*, enables you to search for mediators by location or specialty. The JAMS website, at *www.jamsadr.com*, also enables you to search for a mediator online, as does the website of the Association for Conflict Resolution at *www.acrnet.org/referrals*. On these sites, you can read mediator biographies and find a mediator who has experience or expertise in your type of case. These websites also offer a variety of sample mediation forms, guidelines, and additional articles on mediation.

• If you think a career as a mediator may be right for you, visit the website of the National Association for Community Mediation, at *www.nafcm.org*, for information about mediation training. Your local or state bar association may also offer information about mediation training.

• There are numerous books on the subject of mediation. A good starting point is *The Mediation Process: Practical Strategies for Resolving Conflict,* by C. W. Moore (2nd edition, Jossey-Bass, 1996).

REMEMBER THIS

• Mediation is a process for resolving disputes in which a neutral person, the mediator, facilitates a negotiation between two feuding parties.

• Mediation may help parties, and it will rarely hurt. Parties can generally turn to the court system if mediation doesn't work out.

• Mediation may not be appropriate if the parties want to set a legal precedent, or require a formal determination of right and wrong.

• Mediation is an excellent option for parties who want to solve a dispute without destroying their relationship.

• Mediation is growing in popularity because it is cost-effective and allows parties to craft a unique solution to their problem.

CHAPTER 4

Arbitration

A Flexible Alternative to Litigation

At the 2004 Olympics in Athens, Greece, United States gymnast Paul Hamm won a gold medal in the Men's Individual All-Around competition. But almost immediately after the awards ceremony, he was asked to return his medal when a Korean gymnast claimed that the scores had been improperly calculated. This dispute needed to be handled quickly, and the outcome needed to be final. Going through litigation would have taken too long, and mediation might have ended without an agreement. Luckily, the Court of Arbitration for Sport resolved the matter. In a final ruling that could not be appealed, the Court decided that Hamm should retain his medal. Arbitration saved the day for Paul Hamm; could it be right for your legal issue?

Arbitration is a form of dispute resolution in which an arbitrator hears a dispute in a private, court-like setting and makes a final decision that binds the parties. The parties select the arbitrator, who is often an expert in the subject area of the dispute. The emphasis is on the equity of the situation, and not on the technicalities of the law. For these and many other reasons, arbitration can be a useful tool for resolving disputes. However, it can also pose risks for the unwary.

HOW DOES ARBITRATION DIFFER FROM MEDIATION OR NEGOTIATION?

As we established at the outset of this book, the more formal the process you choose for resolving your dispute, the less control you will have over the outcome. In a negotiation, the parties are in control of the process as well as the outcome. In mediation, the mediator controls the process, but the parties control the outcome. Arbitration is a more formal process than negotiation or mediation. The parties can set the parameters of the arbitration before the hearing, but in the hearing it is the arbitrator—not the parties—who controls both the process and the outcome.

Unlike negotiation and mediation, in which the parties agree on a solution in their mutual interest (or are free not to reach agreement), an arbitrator's decision is valid regardless of whether it satisfies the parties. The American Arbitration Association (AAA) holds the view that an arbitrator's role is to resolve disputes based on their merits. Arbitrators generally do not make an effort to ensure that both sides are happy with their decision. As a result, arbitration is a more adversarial process than mediation or negotiation.

(i) WHEN IS ARBITRATION USED?

Arbitration is used in many different fields, and its use continues to increase. Some contexts in which parties commonly use arbitration include:

- In consumer disputes, to resolve disputes between consumers and companies

- In commercial contexts, to resolve disputes between companies

- In employment and labor disputes, to resolve disputes between workers, or between employers and employees

In addition, almost every major professional sports league uses an arbitration process to resolve disputes.

Arbitration is also increasingly used as a means of resolving international disputes. It is used almost exclusively to settle conflicts arising under the terms of international trade agreements, such as the North American Free Trade Agreement (NAFTA). The United Nations and the International Chamber of Commerce also use arbitration as their primary method of adjudication.

HOW DO CASES GET TO ARBITRATION?

Parties to a dispute can decide to arbitrate for several reasons. This section will explain the various paths that may lead to arbitration.

Voluntary Arbitration

Some arbitration arises when two willing participants agree to the process as a means of resolving their dispute. Parties sometimes take a dispute to arbitration if they have tried negotiation and/or mediation without success. Arbitration is often used as an alternative to litigation.

If you are considering arbitration to resolve your dispute, it can be helpful to consider whether the dispute is primarily about *interests* or about *rights*. If parties can resolve their dispute by reaching a compromise relating to their interests, then negotiation or mediation probably is a more desirable option than

ⓘ THE HISTORY OF ARBITRATION

Arbitration can be traced back to ancient times. The ancient Greeks submitted many disputes to independent third parties who acted as arbitrators. Arbitration was also popular for resolving disputes in ancient Rome. Native Americans used a process similar to arbitration to resolve both intertribal and intra-tribal disputes. In England, arbitration was used in the thirteenth century, before the rise of common law courts. Early English merchants liked arbitration because it allowed them to use their customs as the basis for resolving their disputes.

In the United States, arbitration became widely used during the late nineteenth century. However, courts were reluctant to enforce arbitration awards until the Federal Arbitration Act was passed in 1925.

arbitration. However, if the parties believe their legal rights are at stake in the dispute, then arbitration is probably preferable.

Court-Ordered Arbitration

Prior to trial, courts sometimes order parties to participate in nonbinding arbitration. This means that the parties are not legally bound to comply with the arbitrator's decision, and may continue with litigation if they wish. Judges sometimes order parties to arbitrate because arbitration will give each side a sense of the strength of its case.

The parties to an arbitration can agree to restrict the scope of the arbitrator's decision. For example, parties may require the arbitrator to make an either/or decision between the positions of the two parties. This is known as **pendulum arbitration** or **final-offer arbitration**. In this type of arbitration, the parties have an incentive to submit a moderate final offer in order to increase their chances of winning. Even if the parties do not reach resolution through arbitration, they may be more likely to move towards compromise and reach a settlement after the process has ended. Approximately 80 percent of cases taken to pendulum arbitration are settled without the need for an arbitration hearing.

Arbitration Arising out of a Contract

The majority of arbitrations arise via arbitration clauses. An **arbitration clause** is a section of a contract stating that disputes must be resolved through arbitration. If you have agreed to an arbitration clause in a contract, then you have an **arbitration agreement**. An arbitration clause might look something like this:

> In the event a dispute shall arise between the parties to this contract, it is hereby agreed that the dispute shall be referred to the American Arbitration Association for arbitration in accordance with American Arbitration Association Rules of

Arbitration. The arbitrator's decision shall be final and binding and judgment may be entered thereon.

In the event of unsuccessful challenges to an arbitration award or failure to comply with the award, the prevailing party is ordinarily entitled to costs, including a reasonable attorney's fee for having to compel arbitration or defend or enforce the award.

Arbitrations arising under an arbitration agreement are usually binding, unless otherwise provided in the arbitration clause. This means that the parties are legally obliged to comply with the arbitrator's decision, and have very limited rights to appeal the decision to a court.

If you have agreed to the terms of a credit card, insurance policy, or bank loan, it is likely that you have agreed to an arbitration clause. Often the arbitration clause is included in the fine print of an agreement. Arbitration clauses do not have to be part of your initial agreement with a company. For example, credit card companies may include in your monthly statement an arbitration clause providing that continued use of the credit card constitutes agreement to the arbitration provisions. Arbitration clauses can even be retroactive, applying to disputes that arose before you agreed to the arbitration clause.

Arbitration clauses usually state the procedures to be used in the event of arbitration. Often such clauses state that arbitration will be administered by the American Arbitration Association and subject to its rules.

Consumer rights and employee rights groups often take issue with mandatory arbitration clauses in contracts and agreements. One complaint is that consumers enter into this type of agreement all the time, without having any idea that they have agreed to arbitration. (For more information, see the sidebar on page 73 entitled "The Trouble with Mandatory Arbitration . . .")

Although you are generally bound by any arbitration clause to which you agree, there may be some ways to negate such an agreement. For example, you may be able to argue that your case is not the type of dispute covered by the arbitration clause. Or you may be able to argue that, because an arbitration clause gives one side a large advantage over the other, it is so unconscionable (i.e., unfair) as to be invalid. For example, a California court ruled that an arbitration agreement requiring California consumers to arbitrate their cases in Georgia imposed "unreasonable geographical barriers." The court declared the arbitration clause invalid. Another California court took issue with several parts of an arbitration clause used by AT&T, which among other things prohibited class actions and required proceedings to be kept confidential.

As a result of these cases in California, many standard arbitration agreements exclude California residents. However, other states are not so consumer friendly. If you have entered into a contract with an arbitration clause and you want to get out of it, talk to your attorney about your options.

Arbitration Arising from Employment Agreements

Arbitration is common in the employment context, and typically arises out of arbitration clauses in employment contracts or collectively bargained agreements. There are two common forms of arbitration in the labor context. **Interest arbitration** is used when parties are negotiating a new contract or agreement, and cannot agree on the terms. The parties then call in an arbitrator to break the deadlock and declare the terms of the contract. **Grievance arbitration** is used when an agreement is already in place, and parties are involved in a dispute about the interpretation or application of its terms.

THE LAW ON ARBITRATION

In 1925, Congress passed the Federal Arbitration Act (FAA), which is the cornerstone of arbitration law in the United States. The FAA applies to all arbitrations arising out of transactions that involve interstate commerce. This means that the federal

⚠ THE TROUBLE WITH MANDATORY ARBITRATION . . .

As consumer arbitration has increased in popularity, a debate has evolved between consumer rights groups and business advocates. Consumer rights groups claim that mandatory arbitration circumvents the protections of the legal system, such as the application of the rules of evidence and the right to file class-action lawsuits. They also charge that consumers rarely agree *voluntarily* to arbitration, but instead do so ignorantly when they sign lengthy contracts containing mandatory arbitration clauses buried in legalese. For example, the fine print on an AT&T Pre-Paid phone card obligates the consumer to arbitrate certain disputes, subject to terms listed on a website. The consumer's use of the card constitutes agreement to the arbitration clause.

Business advocates, on the other hand, maintain that arbitration provides an affordable forum for resolving disputes, and that the savings are passed on to consumers. They contend that arbitration does not waive individual rights, and cite research showing that people prefer to resolve their disputes quickly.

Mandatory arbitration contracts in the employment arena are also controversial. Some employees have challenged mandatory arbitration clauses in employment contracts, claiming they never knowingly waived the right to bring disputes to court. Of particular concern to employee rights groups is the ability of companies to prevent workers from suing—including in a class action—in response to such problems as racial, gender-based, age-based, or ethnic discrimination. Some federal courts, such as those in the Third Circuit (which includes Delaware, New Jersey, Pennsylvania, and the U.S. Virgin Islands), have upheld the validity of mandatory arbitration clauses in employee contracts. On the other hand, the Ninth Circuit (which includes California, Oregon, and Washington) has emphasized the need for full disclosure, and in some circumstances has not recognized mandatory arbitration clauses as valid, because employees did not make informed decisions when they agreed to such clauses.

(i) TWO EMPLOYMENT ARBITRATIONS, TWO DIFFERENT RESULTS

In a recent case, three former employees sued the restaurant chain Ryan's Family Steak House for violating the Fair Labor Standards Act, claiming that the company failed to pay minimum wages and overtime. The employees had signed a mandatory arbitration agreement as part of their job application, and the restaurant chain tried to compel arbitration of the dispute. The employees claimed that the arbitration clause could not be enforced.

The appeals court agreed with the employees' arguments, and found that the arbitration agreement could not be enforced for several reasons. The court found that the employees had not known they were waiving their right to a jury trial, because management had not adequately explained the mandatory arbitration clause. In addition, the employees had not had a choice whether to accept the arbitration clause; agreeing to the clause had been a requirement of applying for the job. The employer, meanwhile, could unilaterally modify the agreement without the employees' consent, and choose whether to submit disputes to arbitration. Finally, the judge was troubled by the fact that the arbitration provider received a large percentage of its income from Ryan's Family Steak House.

In another case, *Caley v. Gulfstream*, employees tried to sue their employer, Gulfstream Aerospace Corporation, for violating a variety of laws, including the Fair Labor Standards Act, the Age Discrimination in Employment Act, and ERISA, a law regulating pensions and health plans. In that case, the court found it acceptable that the company had mailed its dispute resolution agreement to the employees, along with an explanation that their continued employment indicated acceptance of the agreement. The court seemed fine with the fact that the agreement required employees to use arbitration but did not require Gulfstream to do so, and with the fact that Gulfstream had the unilateral ability to modify the agreement. The court also did not have a problem with the fact that, for certain claims, the agreement required the employees to give up their right to a jury trial. Gulfstream was successfully able to compel arbitration of the dispute.

law applies to most large companies. The FAA requires courts to recognize and enforce any arbitration clause, just as they enforce any other contract. The FAA also spells out the very narrow grounds on which parties may appeal an arbitration award (for more information, see the section titled "Vacating an Arbitrator's Decision" later in this chapter).

In 1955, the National Conference of Commissioners on Uniform State Laws created the Uniform Arbitration Act (UAA). Thirty-five states have adopted this model legislation, and fourteen other states have passed similar legislation. The UAA establishes the validity of arbitration agreements, and describes how arbitration awards can be corrected, confirmed, or vacated. It also sets out a process for conducting arbitration hearings, to be used unless an arbitration agreement provides otherwise. The UAA is important because it helps the states to make their arbitration laws more consistent.

In 2000, the UAA was amended. The amended act increases the number of procedures that arbitration participants must follow. It also describes rights that parties cannot be forced to waive when entering into arbitration agreements. One important clause of the revised UAA addresses the immunity of arbitrators from lawsuits. This clause states that parties cannot bring a lawsuit against an arbitrator based on his or her decisions, or on the procedures the arbitrator used to reach a decision. This immunity ensures that arbitrators can make decisions without fear of reprisal or lawsuits by the parties. Some jurisdictions already have adopted the revised UAA.

WHY CHOOSE ARBITRATION?

In a journal article published in 1977, former U.S. Supreme Court Chief Justice Warren Burger accurately described why many people prefer arbitration to litigation:

> The notion that most people want black-robed judges, well dressed lawyers and fine paneled courtrooms as the setting to

( ) TALKING TO A LAWYER

Q. The arbitration clause in my agreement with a pest control company states that I, the consumer, must pay all the costs of an arbitration—estimated at $10,000—even if I win the case. This arrangement means I am unlikely to go ahead with my complaint against the company. Is such a clause legal?

A. Yes, although more and more courts are willing to invalidate clauses like this on grounds of unconscionability—particularly if one of the parties to the contract has much more bargaining power than the other. The bottom line, however, is that you should have read the agreement before you signed it, and asked the company to remove this provision. In the future, if a company won't change its contract, find another company.

—Answer by Judge Robert Shenkin,
Court of Common Pleas of Chester County,
West Chester, Pennsylvania

Q. Can arbitration clauses prevent consumers from bringing class actions?

A. A majority of federal courts and a number of state courts have upheld express bans on class actions—in both judicial and arbitration contexts. Other courts, such as in California, have held such provisions to be unconscionable under state law. This debate is likely to come before the U.S. Supreme Court in the near future.

—Answer by Maureen Weston,
Associate Professor,
Pepperdine University School of Law,
Malibu, California

Q. *I read the small print of a contract for my new credit card, and found that the contract includes a mandatory arbitration clause. Is there any way I can avoid agreeing to such a clause?*

A. Probably not, if you want a credit card from that bank—or from almost any bank, since most credit card agreements include such a clause. But you could try complaining to the bank, or looking for another bank or credit card issuer with an agreement more to your liking.

—Answer by Judge Robert Shenkin,
Court of Common Pleas of Chester County,
West Chester, Pennsylvania

resolve their dispute is not correct. People with problems, like people with pains, want relief, and they want it as quickly and inexpensively as possible.

As Chief Justice Burger suggests, arbitration is popular in part because, compared to litigation, it can save parties time and money. It also offers participants more flexibility and control than litigation.

The benefits of arbitration are discussed in more detail below. However, bear in mind that these benefits exist only if both parties agree to arbitration in good faith.

Enforcing Your Rights

When you need to enforce your rights against a more powerful party, arbitration can be preferable to negotiation or mediation.

An example will help to illustrate this point. Suppose Margot is a medical student who lives in a large residential building near campus. In January, Margot's building is undergoing construction and the noise from the drilling prevents her from studying at home. If Margot tries to resolve this problem through negotiation or mediation, the building's management will have little incentive to reach an agreement with her. The parties don't share

ⓘ INTEREST-BASED ARBITRATION

For the most part, arbitrators do not consider the *interests* of the parties to a dispute; instead, they make a decision based on the parties' *rights*. However, in **interest-based arbitration**, which is used for some collective-bargaining agreements such as professional baseball salary disputes, the arbitrator does look at the interests of both sides. In interest-based arbitration of a dispute arising from a collectively bargained agreement, both sides generally make a final offer, and then the arbitrator chooses between the two. This method allows the parties some control over the outcome.

mutual interests regarding the construction, and Margot's best alternative is to sue the building. This is a poor alternative for Margot because she cannot afford an attorney, and she wants the noise to stop soon so she can study for her upcoming exams. A lawsuit would be costly, and it certainly would not end within four months. Furthermore, Margot knows that her building has a lengthy wait-list of potential tenants, so threatening to move out won't afford her any bargaining leverage. Finally, many of the other tenants in her building aren't home during the day. Since the noise doesn't bother them, they aren't interested in a rent strike or petition.

Margot's lease contains an arbitration clause that requires her to file complaints with the tenant's board for her building, and specifies that arbitration is the mandatory procedure for resolving disputes. If Margot makes a complaint, the tenant's board will arrange for arbitration. The arbitrator will rely on the terms of Margot's lease and on local laws governing nuisance to reach a decision, rather than looking to the parties' interests. Since Margot is looking to enforce her rights—as opposed to the management company, which is simply looking to advance its interests—arbitration will be a satisfying forum for Margot to resolve her dispute.

ⓘ THERE'S A PRECEDENT

In some industries, arbitrators sometimes rely on precedent in making their decisions. For example, arbitrators within self-contained trade groups sometimes distribute opinions to their members, which are relied upon like precedents. The Court of Arbitration for Sport, which is mentioned in the opening paragraph of this chapter, acts as a supreme court within the world of international sports arbitration. Its opinions are used as precedents, and are often treated as the equivalent of law in affiliated arbitration hearings. On the less glamorous end of things, the National Grain and Feed Association—a trade association that represents and provides services for more than one thousand grain- and feed-related commercial businesses—hears many similar cases within its trade groups, which increases the likelihood that it will make similar decisions in similar cases.

Avoiding Setting a Precedent

In the public court system, most cases become legal precedent. This means that when a case is decided, future litigants can cite that case in their favor, and courts must try to make rulings consistent with that decision.

On the other hand, arbitration decisions generally bind only the parties in the case at hand, and do not affect future disputes. This can be advantageous to parties who wish to minimize the chances of a court ruling against them in similar cases in the future. The wish to avoid a precedent-setting decision often creates an important incentive for parties to settle a matter.

Keep in mind that, because most arbitration proceedings create no precedent, it would not be surprising for two different arbitrators to arrive at two completely different decisions in cases involving the exact same facts. For example, suppose Karolyn and Isabella are both small-business owners and members of the Rhode Island Chamber of Commerce. Both suffered damages to their businesses, which occupy the same street, due to power outages arising from a snowstorm. Both initiated arbitration hearings against the power company, and were assigned different arbitrators. Karolyn received compensation equal to 75 percent of the amount she sought, while Isabella received no compensation at all.

This example illustrates the uncertainty arising from the fact that arbitrations are not bound by precedent. Even if arbitrators are aware of decisions made in similar or identical cases, they are completely free to rule differently if they believe their decision will bring about the best outcome in the case before them. This problem is complicated by the fact that most arbitrators are not required to supply reasons for their decisions. The unpredictability resulting from lack of precedent is an oft-cited criticism of arbitration.

Confidentiality

You may also benefit from the confidentiality of arbitration. When a lawsuit is filed in court, it becomes a matter of public record accessible to anyone. In particular, journalists are free to write stories about the decision. For many people, fears of negative publicity make this a frightening prospect. In contrast, the parties to arbitration can agree to keep the agreement reached in arbitration confidential. Decisions in arbitrations generally are not made available to the public.

For example, suppose that Allison, a dentist, is accused by her patient, Will, of dental malpractice. Regardless of whether the allegations are true, public knowledge of such a lawsuit could be detrimental to Allison's career, as many of her patients might choose to see another dentist. However, if the case is heard in arbitration instead of in court, Allison's patients might never find out about the accusation of malpractice, or the outcome of the case.

However, arbitration may not always shield you from the public eye. Consider the case of NFL football player Terrell Owens of the Philadelphia Eagles, who was suspended from playing football for part of a season as punishment for unsportsmanlike conduct. The disciplinary matter went to arbitration. But while the hearing itself was private, the general public was well aware that the arbitrator eventually upheld Owens' suspension.

Finality

For many commercial parties, one of the most attractive aspects of arbitration is the fact that arbitration can resolve disputes with finality. Negotiation and mediation are generally viewed as nonbinding, so both sides have the option of walking out before an agreement is reached—and even after an agreement is reached, unless the agreement is approved by a court. One reason that litigation is so expensive and so draining is that either side can appeal the judge's verdict to a higher court. Appeal proceedings can require a great deal of time and money.

(i) NONBINDING ARBITRATION

Not all forms of arbitration emphasize finality. Parties can agree to enter **nonbinding arbitration**, also known as **advisory arbitration**, in which they are not bound by an arbitrator's decision. If parties agree to nonbinding arbitration, an arbitrator will hear their case, but his or her opinion will be advisory in nature. This means that the parties may proceed with the case however they choose after the opinion is handed down—for example, they may agree to adhere to the advisory opinion, settle the case under different terms, or decide to continue with litigation. Nonbinding arbitration can provide you with an objective opinion about what will happen if you pursue a case further. Moreover, since nonbinding arbitration offers you a preview of what a court might say, it may make it easier to reach a settlement with the other side.

Many court systems throughout the country order litigants to pursue nonbinding arbitration. The parties must attend such arbitration, but are not bound by its result, and can continue to litigate their cases if they choose.

▶ ## AN EXCEPTION TO THE
FINALITY RULE

Self-contained trade groups often provide that decisions made in arbitration can be appealed to committees within the group.

In contrast, a single arbitration hearing can produce a final decision. Once parties have agreed to binding arbitration, they must follow through with it. And once the arbitrator has made a decision, the parties are required to abide by it. Appealing an arbitrator's decision to the courts is only allowed in very limited circumstances. (For more information, see the section titled "Vacating an Arbitrator's Decision" later in this chapter.)

An arbitrator usually files his or her decision with the court within twelve months; the court then confirms it, and the decision becomes an order of the court. The arbitration decision is then enforceable. This means that if a person refuses to adhere to the decision, he or she can be found in contempt of court, fined, or even imprisoned.

The finality of arbitration is a huge advantage for many commercial parties. The fact that a case can be resolved after a single arbitration hearing can make arbitration much cheaper than litigation. It also means that cases are resolved more quickly. Prevailing parties can receive compensation more quickly, and both sides can move on from the case.

Expertise

For many commercial parties, another advantage of arbitration is that arbitrators often have expertise in specific industries. Such expertise may include substantive knowledge of an industry, its customs, and its culture.

For example, suppose that Rita, a realtor, shows Kristin a house. Kristin likes the house, but instead of calling Rita when she decides to purchase it, Kristin contacts Scott, a second realtor. A dispute later arises between Scott and Rita over who is entitled to the commission, and the matter goes to arbitration. Because the arbitrator, Debby, has years of experience in the field of real estate, she understands the nuances of the regulations that affect the case. Specifically, she knows that real estate regulations generally provide that the first broker who shows a client a house is considered the **procuring cause** of the sale, and is thus entitled to the commission. Debby's familiarity with this industry custom gives her a better understanding than a judge might have of how best to handle the situation. She is also likely to have a better understanding of the parties' expectations.

Avoiding Juries

Arbitration disputes are heard by an arbitrator or panel of arbitrators; arbitration agreements prevent juries from hearing disputes. This can be attractive for companies suffering from a bad reputation (think Enron). Many defendants believe that arbitrators award lower amounts than juries. And in fact, a survey by the National Working Rights Institute (available at *www.workrights.org/current/cd_arbitration.html*) has shown that average jury awards in employment cases are higher than average awards in arbitration. Employees and consumer plaintiffs sometimes dislike arbitration clauses for this reason.

Arbitrations and Jurisdiction

Arbitration can be useful when a dispute is between people or companies from different countries. For example, the World Anti-Doping Agency requires that doping disputes be resolved by the Court of Arbitration for Sport rather than by courts of individual countries. Otherwise, it fears, cases could be decided differently in countries with different laws, and judges could be biased toward litigants from their own countries. For the same reasons, arbitration is commonly used for international business disputes.

In the United States, arbitration can help parties to avoid time-consuming and costly disputes regarding which court has appropriate jurisdiction to hear a case.

SELECTING AN ARBITRATOR

Once you have decided to resolve a dispute through arbitration, you will need to select an arbitrator. The arbitrator you choose generally has complete authority over the case. Because of this, it is important to choose the right arbitrator; often a significant percentage of the time spent preparing for arbitration proceedings is spent choosing an arbitrator.

You will want to choose an arbitrator (or arbitrators) whom you believe will be fair and impartial. In order to ensure impartiality, it is common for cases to be heard by a panel of three arbitrators, with each side selecting one arbitrator and those two arbitrators selecting the third.

Some critics of arbitration suggest that industry experts who act as arbitrators may be more sympathetic to the industry than to individuals. For example, in a dispute about home construction, an arbitration panel composed of contractors and architects may be more sympathetic to a contractor than to a consumer. On the other hand, it can be argued that members of a profession are more likely to protect their professional reputations by punishing true misconduct where they see it.

Allegations of bias have also arisen in situations where arbitrators depend on one particular client or company for repeat business. In such circumstances, the arbitrator may have some incentive to act more favorably toward the party that arbitrates frequently. For example, if a substantial amount of an arbitrator's business involves arbitrating consumer disputes for ABC Incorporated, he or she may be more likely to find in favor of ABC Incorporated, to the detriment of consumers.

In an effort to ensure impartiality and proper conduct, the American Bar Association and the American Arbitration Association have adopted standards of ethics for arbitrators. These standards, listed in the ABA/AAA Code of Ethics for Arbitrators in Commercial Disputes, obligate arbitrators to inform both sides of any potential conflicts of interest. If proper disclosures are made, parties will be aware of the potential for prejudice.

The standards also require arbitrators keep confidential any information learned in arbitration hearings. In addition, trade associations that provide arbitration for their members often have their own codes of ethics that are binding on their members.

Arbitrators need not be judges or lawyers. While many people prefer to have retired judges as arbitrators, it is common for arbitrators to be selected based on other qualifications, such as expertise in a particular field. For example, suppose scientists Micah and Milena become involved in a dispute while developing devices to help paralyzed people write. Micah claims that Milena has copied his invention and infringed his patent. An arbitrator with expertise in prosthetics may be the most qualified "judge" for this type of dispute, as he or she can apply specialized knowledge of the industry to determine the correct outcome. Often such experts are not full-time arbitrators, but practice in a field related to the controversy.

There is no licensing standard or certification required for arbitrators. However, individual associations that provide arbitration, such as the International Association of Professional Debt Arbitrators, have their own internal certification requirements.

If you do not want to choose an arbitrator yourself, or if the parties cannot agree on an arbitrator, you can turn the selection process over to a nonprofit or for-profit organization. In addition to helping with the selection process, many organizations offer help in administering arbitration hearings, and can provide rules for arbitration procedures.

▶ LISTS OF ARBITRATORS

Even if you intend to select your own arbitrator, it can be helpful to peruse the lists provided by a nonprofit or for-profit organization that facilitates arbitration. For example, the AAA has a list of over fifty thousand arbitrators, most of whom have been nominated by prominent members of their respective industries and professions.

(i) ARBITRATORS AND JUDGES

Judges:

- must obey the rules of procedure in their courts
- must follow precedent
- must provide reasons for their decisions, in the interest of making the decision-making process transparent
- are public officers, who may be accountable at the ballot box

Arbitrators have much more flexibility than judges. They:

- follow the rules of arbitration, which usually are more flexible than the rules of court
- are not bound by prior decisions
- do not have to give reasons for their decisions

In order to help you select an arbitrator, organizations that facilitate arbitration will send both sides a list of arbitrators qualified in the area of the dispute, and will include information about the arbitrators' backgrounds. Both sides will then have time to read through the list, mark off the names of arbitrators they are unwilling to use, and order the remaining names according to preference. The parties then return their lists to the facilitating organization, which will try to appoint an arbitrator based on everyone's preferences. If the parties cannot agree on an arbitrator, the facilitator will appoint one. Provider organizations work to make sure that their arbitrators are impartial, with no conflicts of interest in the cases to which they are assigned.

The Arbitration Process

Arbitration clauses in contracts usually must set out the procedures to be used in an arbitration hearing. One of the great advantages of arbitration is that parties can create an arbitration process that meets their unique needs. They can, for example, agree to participate in binding or nonbinding arbitration. They can decide whether the rules of evidence that apply in court should apply in the arbitration hearing. Parties can take steps to make the procedures of the arbitration more or less formal, as they prefer. They can limit the decision-making discretion of the arbitrator and can also agree to limit the involvement of lawyers, or agree that lawyers should not be involved in the arbitration at all. Parties can agree on the timing of arbitration, and can place limits on the length of preparation time and the length of the hearing.

All these details regarding arbitration can be established when the arbitration clause in a contract is drafted. If two or more parties negotiate a contract, all sides have the chance to negotiate the wording and content of the arbitration clause, and can thus design an arbitration process that is fair for everyone. Of course, if one party drafts the contract and the other party simply signs it—as is often the case with contracts entered into by consumers and employees—then the arbitration process is likely to hold an advantage for the drafting party.

Despite the potential for creativity, many arbitration clauses reference the procedures established by the American Arbitration Association. In the standard arbitration format established by the AAA, an arbitration hearing feels like a miniature trial. Generally, hearings begin with a brief opening statement. Normally the party making the claim presents its case first. Both sides then describe how they think the dispute should be resolved. Witnesses are questioned by both sides, as well as by the arbitrator, and other evidence may be introduced. Finally, each side has a chance to present a closing statement to the arbitrator.

In conducting a case, the arbitrator has much more flexibility than a judge. For example, the arbitrator may visit sites outside the hearing room, call expert witnesses, seek out additional evidence, actively participate in the hearing, and decide appropriate remedies.

After a hearing, the arbitrator generally has thirty days to announce his or her decision. The arbitrator's decision is called

( ) TALKING TO A LAWYER

Q. I've read that an arbitration agreement can specify the laws to be followed in the arbitration. Does this mean that an arbitrator can apply the laws of another state?

A. Yes. One of the advantages of arbitration is that the parties can set their own rules. Of course, that can be a terrible disadvantage if one of the parties sets the rules and the other party simply accepts those rules without really knowing or understanding them.

For example, if you sign a credit card application or an equipment finance lease with a bank, the agreement might allow the bank to submit a dispute to arbitration in a location near the bank's headquarters, or in some bank-friendly jurisdiction far away from where you live. This could make it very inconvenient, if not impossible, for you to contest the bank's claims in arbitration. Similarly, when you use the Internet and are asked to accept or reject certain conditions in order to use a particular website, those conditions might include an agreement to arbitrate in some distant location. You should always read everything in a document before you sign it. Be particularly careful to read everything in a small font size—the dreaded "fine print."

> —Answer by Judge Robert Shenkin,
> Court of Common Pleas of Chester County,
> West Chester, Pennsylvania

Q. I've read that arbitration clauses are often combined with forum selection and choice-of-law clauses. Is it true that these clauses could compel me to arbitrate in a strange private forum thousands of miles from home, and that arbitrators may decide my case based on the law of a state I have never even visited?

A. These types of clauses may—and probably should—be challenged as unconscionable. However, in the 1991 case *Carnival Cruise Lines v.*

Shute, the Supreme Court upheld forum selection clauses similar to the type you describe. Thus, as a matter of contract, other courts are also likely to uphold such provisions.

—Answer by Maureen Weston,
Associate Professor,
Pepperdine University School of Law,
Malibu, California

the **award**. The arbitrator may issue a **reasoned award**, in which he or she sets out the reasons for the decision, or an **abbreviated** award, which simply states the decision and does not provide reasons for it. After the arbitrator has made a decision, his or her authority over the case ends—unless both sides agree otherwise.

VACATING AN ARBITRATOR'S DECISION

Ordinarily, arbitration proceedings are final and cannot be appealed. There are circumstances, however, in which you can ask a court to **vacate** or **disqualify** an arbitrator's decision. If a court vacates an award, it means that the ruling has no effect. Sometimes the court will order that a new arbitration take place to resolve the dispute.

The Federal Arbitration Act requires that a request to a court to vacate or disqualify an arbitrator's decision must be made within three months of the award. According to the Federal Arbitration Act, an award can be vacated

• if the arbitration was won by corruption, fraud, or undue means;
• if the arbitrator was biased or corrupt;
• if the arbitrators were guilty of misconduct or misbehavior that prejudiced the rights of any party; or
• if the arbitrators exceeded their powers.

For example, a New York court decided that TV arbitrator Judge Judy had exceeded her power in a property case, because she had taken into account the child custody arrangements of the parties. The court held that Judge Judy's decision was outside the scope of the parties' arbitration agreement.

The Federal Arbitration Act does not provide a standard for determining whether an award can be vacated due to arbitrator bias, and courts have not been consistent in their determinations of what constitutes bias. Many courts will find an arbitrator to be biased if a reasonable person, hearing the circumstances of the case in question, would believe that arbitrator to be biased. In the case *Commonwealth Coatings Corp. v. Continental Casualty Co.*, the Supreme Court found bias where an arbitrator had previously worked as a contractor for one of the parties, and had failed to disclose this relationship.

Courts can also modify an arbitrator's award on the basis of clerical or numerical error—for example, when an arbitrator makes a miscalculation in his or her computation of the award.

Finally, judges will vacate an award if there has been "manifest disregard for the law," which occurs on rare occasions when an arbitrator is "aware of a clear governing legal principle . . . but [has] refused or declined to apply it." This doctrine only applies in cases where the arbitrator goes beyond mere error, and intentionally disregards the law.

However, courts are not able to review the substantive content of a decision made in a binding arbitration. This means that, if an arbitrator makes a legal mistake that falls short of "manifest disregard for the law," the court cannot overturn his or her decision.

THE WORLD AT YOUR FINGERTIPS

• Some sample arbitration decisions are available on the website of the Court of Arbitration for Sport, at *www.tas-cas.org/en/juris/frmjur.htm.*

• More information about arbitration, including national listings of rated, certified arbitrators in various industries, can be found at the American Arbitration Association's website at *www.adr.org*. You can also find qualified and recommended arbitrators in your area by visiting *www.jamsadr.com* and *www.acrnet.org/referrals*.

• The website of the National Arbitration Forum, at *www.arbforum.com*, features articles on arbitration and sample arbitration clauses.

• To view the latest version of the Code of Ethics for Arbitrators in Commercial Disputes, promulgated by the American Bar Association and the American Arbitration Association, visit *www.adr.org/sp.asp?id=21962*.

• For an international perspective on arbitration, including case law, articles, and links to current arbitration news, visit the website of the International Institute for Conflict Prevention and Resolution at *www.cpradr.org*.

• To learn more about why consumer rights groups oppose some arbitration practices, visit the website of the National Consumer Law Center at *www.consumerlaw.org/initiatives/model/arbitration.shtml*.

• If you want to know more about arbitration in the labor context, check out *Labor Arbitration: What You Need To Know*, by Robert Coulson (5th edition, American Arbitration Association, 2003).

REMEMBER THIS

• Arbitration is a form of dispute resolution in which an arbitrator hears a dispute in a private, court-like setting.

• Arbitration can be binding or nonbinding. In binding arbitration, the parties are obliged to comply with the decision of the arbitrator. In nonbinding arbitration, parties are free to comply with the arbitrator's decision, reach a different settlement, or continue with litigation.

• Arbitration is voluntary; both sides must agree to have their dispute resolved through arbitration. However, many people agree to binding arbitration unwittingly, by consenting to an agreement that includes an arbitration clause.

• One of the advantages of arbitration is that the parties can create an arbitration process that meets their unique needs. Parties can select an arbitrator, and decide on the rules that will apply to their proceeding.

• In most cases, arbitration is final; there is no appeal. However, you may ask a court to vacate an arbitration decision if it results from bias or corruption, or if an arbitrator has exceeded the scope of an arbitration clause.

CHAPTER 5

Small-Claims Court

The "Fast Food" of the Legal System

Nancy loved her apartment. Her place was close to the train, and she had a great relationship with her neighbors. The one thing Nancy didn't like was her landlord, Trent. Trent neglected his tenants. He once refused to fix a broken lock at the building's entrance until a tenant threatened to call the city. Nancy always tried her best to avoid any conflicts with him.

When Nancy was transferred to a new job in a different city, she moved out. She asked for the return of her $1,400 security deposit. But Trent only returned $560 to her, stating that the other $840 was needed for repairs. Nancy was furious, and disputed the claims. Trent refused to budge. Nancy's friend suggested mediation, but Nancy didn't trust Trent to negotiate in good faith. She called a lawyer, who told her that filing a lawsuit and going through a trial would likely cost more than the $840 for which she would be suing. But then the lawyer suggested small-claims court. The next day, Nancy went to her county courthouse and filed an action in small-claims court seeking the return of her $840, plus five years' worth of interest. Shortly thereafter, Nancy was awarded a judgment in the amount of $910, which was the amount of the security deposit she was owed, plus interest.

Small-claims court is an informal and relatively inexpensive forum for resolving certain types of small disputes. There are typically no lawyers involved, the cases last an hour or less, and there isn't a jury.

Inexpensive, informal, and quick? It certainly sounds enticing. But there are a lot of factors you should consider before deciding that small-claims court is the right venue for resolving your dispute.

STATE LAWS

Small-claims courts are state regulated, and are not governed by a federal system. This means that the rules, regulations, and limitations of small-claims court are controlled by fifty individual states, and differ from state to state. Small-claims courts usually are a part of your local district, county, or municipal court, and have different names in different places—in some states and counties they may be called **county courts** or **magistrate's**

⚠️ **EVERY STATE IS DIFFERENT**

In this chapter, we try to provide general information that applies to small-claims courts in every state. However, each state has its own procedures. If you are going to go to small-claims court, you must learn about the procedures applicable in your particular location. Sometimes there are different procedures for different areas in the same state. A large city might have one name for its small-claims court, and a rural area might have another; these two locations might even follow different procedures. In this chapter we will discuss procedures that are common in many small-claims courts. But remember: No single court will be exactly like the courts in our examples.

Every state has a trial court of general jurisdiction. If you're going to small-claims court, this is the court you're attempting to avoid. The **trial court of general jurisdiction** is where all kinds of lawsuits are heard, including cases involving large sums of money. In many states this court will be called the **district court**, which is the name given to trial courts in the federal system. But this type of court can also be known as the **superior court**, or the **court of common pleas**. In New York State, the trial court of general jurisdiction is called the **Supreme Court**. There are many more types of courts and names for those courts. You can find more information about trial courts of general jurisdiction in Chapter 6.

ⓘ TAX COURTS ARE THE EXCEPTION

There is one exception to the rule that small-claims courts are regulated by the states, and that is the federal tax court, which does hear small claims. A case will qualify for the small-case division of the federal tax court if the disputed amount is $50,000 or less in any one tax year, including penalties.

The procedures followed in the small-claims division of the federal tax court are similar to those followed in other small-claims courts: the court is informal, the trial lasts less than an hour, and the parties usually don't need lawyers, though they can have them if they choose. Many cases settle before trial; generally the IRS will offer to settle for a smaller amount than is allegedly owed.

---

courts. Still, most states administer their small-claims court systems in a similar fashion. The information in this chapter is designed to help you regardless of where you live.

If you have specific questions about the small-claims court in your state, contact the small-claims court clerk of the district in which you are located. (See "The World at Your Fingertips" section at the end of this chapter for a Web address where you can link to the small-claims courts in your state.)

LAWYERS IN SMALL-CLAIMS COURT

In most states, you may have a lawyer represent you in small-claims court if you wish. But just because you are allowed to bring a lawyer, doesn't always mean you should. In many cases it is not in your best interest to hire a lawyer, because the money you are seeking to recover can be lost in legal fees. In fact, most people in small-claims courts do not have lawyers. Happily, some studies show that small-claims plaintiffs representing themselves fare just as well as those with legal representation.

( ) TALKING TO A LAWYER

Q. In my state, lawyers are allowed in small-claims court. Won't I always be at an advantage if I hire one for my case?

A. Yes, but that doesn't mean you should. You might be more likely to win your case, but the cost of the lawyer might be more than the amount you collect from the other side. If your state provides an absolute right to appeal, you should consider representing yourself in small-claims court, after first trying to work out the dispute by negotiation or mediation. Then consult a lawyer only if the result in small-claims court is not satisfactory, or if the other side appeals. If you are not satisfied with the result in small-claims court, consult with a lawyer right away. The period within which you may take further action, such as appealing, might be very short. And if the other side appeals, you might need to take action very quickly or have your case dismissed.

—Answer by Judge Robert Shenkin,
Court of Common Pleas of Chester County,
West Chester, Pennsylvania

A few states do not allow lawyers into small-claims court at all. In addition, a few states allow only the **plaintiff** (the party who initiates a lawsuit) to use a lawyer if the **defendant** (the person being sued) chooses to use one first. In some states, lawyers are only allowed in small-claims court with the permission of the judge.

CASES SUITABLE FOR SMALL-CLAIMS COURT

Small-claims courts primarily handle cases involving relatively small amounts of money. Each of the fifty states sets an upper limit (called the **jurisdictional limit**) on the amount of money that can be sought in small-claims courts. Typically the jurisdictional limit is between $2,000 and $7,000, but some states have limits as high as $15,000. These might seem like substantial amounts of money, but they are relatively small in comparison to the sums disputed in district or federal courts.

If you are seeking an amount that exceeds the small-claims limit for your state, you may still bring a case in small-claims court. But by suing in small-claims court, you will give up your claim to any amount over the jurisdictional limit. For instance, if you're a homeowner in California who believes a contractor owes you $7,000, you may only claim and recover up to $5,000 in small-claims court. You can't come back later and demand the other $2,000—one bite is all you get. If you are in this situation, you'll need to decide whether it's more important for you to go to small-claims court to pursue some of the money, or bring your case in a higher court for a chance at all of the money. In this example, this decision might mean the difference between getting

---

 **BEWARE OF EMPTY POCKETS**

If a person has no money or assets, he or she may be **judgment-proof**. This means that he or she will not be able to pay you even if you win the case, and you might end up with no money. You can try to find out whether the person or business you want to sue has money or assets, whether they are close to bankruptcy, and whether other judgments have been made against them that have not been paid. To find this information, you might wish to review real estate records and court records. The INeed2Know website has some useful information about how to search for such information; visit *www.ineed2know.org/business/asset-search.htm*.

If the opposing party is judgment-proof, you should think twice before pursuing a lawsuit that will cost you money and time, and may result in a judgment that you will never be able to collect. Remember that winning a case in small-claims court is not the same thing as getting paid.

▶ **EXPLORE YOUR OPTIONS**

As you know from reading the previous chapters on negotiation, mediation, and arbitration, you have other options for resolving your dispute besides small-claims court. It is important to understand that, just because you *can* resolve a matter in small-claims court, it might not always be in your best interest to do so. In particular, you may want to consider whether you want the matter discussed in public, how the case might affect your reputation, and whether there will be opportunities for you and the other side to work together in the future.

In particular, you may wish to ask your local small-claims court clerk for help with mediation. Mediation of a small-claims case is mandatory in some areas of the country. In others, it is easily accessible on a voluntary basis, either right in the courthouse or at a nearby community mediation center. Contact a mediation center to enlist its help in bringing the other party to the table. (Chapter 3 contains more detailed information about mediation.)

$5,000 within a couple of months, or $7,000 a year or two down the road, minus attorney's fees and court costs.

In order to find out the applicable limits in your state, contact the small-claims clerk of your local court. Most states provide this information online. (For more information, see the section titled "The World at Your Fingertips" at the end of this chapter.)

Common matters handled in small-claims court include disputes involving

- debts;
- repayment of loans;
- failure to provide agreed-upon services;
- breach or cancellation of contracts;
- minor personal injuries;
- breach of warranty—for example, when a purchased product is defective or not as advertised;

- property damage;
- evictions; and
- return of property—for example, when a person borrows something and does not return it.

However, not all disputes can be settled in small-claims court. Types of cases that generally *cannot* be brought in small-claims courts include

- criminal matters;
- class-action lawsuits;
- cases arising from traffic violations;
- divorce proceedings;
- bankruptcy filings;
- name change requests;
- guardianship requests; and
- any kind of lawsuit against a state, the federal government, or a federal agency.

WHERE CAN YOU SUE?

Where should you bring a case in small-claims court? The answer is that it typically depends on where the person you are suing (the **defendant**) lives or works. Generally, you can sue someone close to their home or job. In some cases you can also bring suit in the area where the disputed activity took place. For instance, in a case about stolen property, you can sue where the theft took place. In a breach-of-contract case, you can sue where the contract was signed. And in a case arising from personal injury, you can generally sue where the accident occurred. Note that if the defendant doesn't live or do business in your state, and the matter in dispute did not take place in your state, then you will have to bring suit in the state where the defendant lives or does business, or in a state where you can prove a connection exists.

For example, suppose Katharine lives and works in Brussels, Illinois. She owns a riding stable and provides horseback-riding lessons to local children and summer tourists. One tourist,

⚠️ STATUTES OF LIMITATIONS

A statute of limitations is a law that establishes a time frame within which you must file a case (the term is often also used to refer to the time frame itself). Different states have different statutes of limitations for different kinds of cases. For example, if you are suing to recover money for a breach of contract, the statute of limitations might be three years. This means that if you do not file a lawsuit within three years of the alleged breach, you will no longer be allowed to bring suit at all.

If something has happened to you that you think may give rise to a lawsuit, you should act without delay. For purposes of the statute of limitations, the clock usually starts ticking when the damage or injury occurs, but sometimes won't start until you become aware of the damage or injury. If you have waited a while before bringing suit, you might want to consult with a lawyer to find out if the statute of limitations will pose a problem in your case.

Bernard, injures his toe while participating in the lessons. Bernard is a resident of Ann Arbor, Michigan. His toe injuries cost him a total of $2,200 in medical expenses, and he wants to sue Katharine in small-claims court in Ann Arbor. However, because Katharine does not live or conduct business in Ann Arbor, and because the injury didn't occur in Ann Arbor or anywhere else in Michigan, he cannot do so. If Bernard wants to sue Katharine, he must do so in the small-claims court near Brussels, Illinois.

SMALL-CLAIMS COURT PROCEDURES

Once you determine that your case is appropriate for small-claims court and where to file, you will need to follow the steps required by the courts in your state. While the applicable procedures vary from state to state, most states require that plaintiffs

1. file a complaint and pay a filing fee, and
2. **serve** (i.e., notify) the defendant, and submit proof of notification to the small-claims court.

This section will discuss these steps in more detail.

Filing a Complaint

To file a complaint, you will need to obtain the proper complaint form from the small-claims court in your area. On the form, you will typically need to write your name and address, and the name and address of the person or business against whom you are filing the claim. You will need to know if the defendant is an individual or a corporation; this information is generally available from your state government, and usually can be obtained online. Don't assume that just because you are dealing with a business you should sue in the name of that business. For example, if you think that Mike's Hardware Store owes you money, but Mike's Hardware Store is not a corporation, you will need to find out the name of the business owner (probably someone named Mike) and sue that particular person. But if the business is a corporation, you will want to list the corporation as the defendant. On the complaint form, you will also have to provide the amount of money in dispute, and list the reasons you are seeking payment from the defendant.

Be clear and concise when you give your reasons for seeking payment. You may want to use numbered paragraphs or bullet points. Remember: The more clearly you provide the relevant information, the more likely a judge will be to understand the basis of your complaint before the hearing.

In many jurisdictions, complaint forms are available on the Internet. Some states even allow you to fill out and submit complaint forms online. Most states' complaint forms look similar. The filing fees vary by state, but generally are around $30.

When you file your complaint form with the small-claims

court clerk, he or she will provide you with the date and time at which your case will be heard. Most small-claim courts will set a trial date that is thirty to ninety days after your complaint is filed.

Notifying the Defendant

After you have filed a claim with the appropriate small-claims court, you must notify the defendant that a case has been filed against him or her. Occasionally the court itself will take care of sending notice, but more often you will be responsible for providing notice to the defendant. You must notify the defendant through a formal legal process called **service**. Service procedures require that the defendant be given a copy of the complaint within a certain time period; the specific time limit is

(i) COUNTERCLAIMS

If you decide to sue a person in small-claims court, that person may be able to bring a counterclaim, or countersuit, against you. A **counterclaim** is a claim by the defendant against the plaintiff. For example, suppose Nancy moves out of her apartment and files suit against her landlord in small-claims court. The landlord may file a counterclaim asserting that she owes him money because she caused damage to the carpet in the apartment. If Nancy sues for the return of $1,400, and the landlord has spent $1,900 to replace the carpeting, then he may countersue Nancy for the additional $500.

If a defendant brings a counterclaim against you, you will have to defend yourself against that claim at the hearing. If the other side seeks an amount that is above the jurisdictional limit of the small-claims court, then the case can be transferred to the trial court of general jurisdiction. Trial courts are still state courts, but they are much more formal, and both sides generally have attorneys.

( ) TALKING TO A LAWYER

Q. I am a small-business owner being sued in small-claims court by a former employee. Is it advantageous for me to countersue so that the case moves to regular civil court?

A. Maybe. But if the case is transferred to a trial court, you will need a lawyer, and the cost of a lawyer might be more than the amount in dispute. Your former employee might also get a lawyer, and decide that the value of his or her case exceeds the limit on small-claims cases in your jurisdiction. If that happens, you could find yourself in a much more precarious position than when the matter was in small-claims court. Of course, you cannot file a counterclaim against your former employee without a reasonable basis for doing so, and the desire to move your case to a different court does not itself constitute a valid basis for filing a counterclaim. Rather, you will need to have some real basis for claiming that your former employee is liable to you.

—Answer by Judge Robert Shenkin,
Court of Common Pleas of Chester County,
West Chester, Pennsylvania

determined by the local small-claims court, but is usually approximately thirty days. When the document has been appropriately delivered, the defendant has been **served.**

In order to serve a defendant with a document, you need to follow the exact procedures established for your jurisdiction. Sometimes you can simply mail the complaint to the defendant, but usually ordinary mail is not sufficient. Certified or registered mail is generally required, in which case you must get a return receipt signed by the defendant to prove that he or she actually received the document. Other courts require that someone physically present the defendant with a summons or copy of the complaint. Ask the clerk in your small-claims court what service procedures are required.

These formal requirements for delivering documents to defendants exist for a good reason. Bringing a lawsuit, even in small-claims court, is a serious matter. Service rules are designed to ensure that defendants are notified of lawsuits, and thus have the chance to defend themselves in court.

PREPARING YOUR CASE

Once the defendant has been properly notified about the case and a court date is set, both sides should begin preparing their cases. In preparing your case, consider what information the judge will need in order to rule in your favor, and how you can present this information clearly. Bear in mind that the judge might not be a lawyer; in some states a law degree is not required in order to become a small-claims court judge. However, even if the judge is not a lawyer, he or she will almost always have some type of legal training and will have heard many, many cases similar to yours.

Evidence

Good, well-prepared evidence is your best friend in small-claims court, and failure to provide necessary evidence will destroy your chances of winning. Trials in small-claims court are brief. Both parties have a limited time to tell the judge their side of the story, and it can be difficult for a judge to make a ruling based solely on each person's version of events. That is why it is important to provide the judge with evidence that supports your story and proves your case.

There are different forms of evidence that you may bring to trial to support your case. The most common forms of evidence are:

• **Eyewitnesses.** These are people who saw firsthand the events affecting your case. For example, in a case about a car accident, you might have an eyewitness who saw one car hit another, and noted the license plate numbers.

• **Photographs.** The best photos are clear and properly labeled. For example, in a case about breach of contract for shoddy construction, you might bring photos showing a leaky roof and cracked walls.

• **Written contracts or other written documents.** Written documents are very helpful in any breach-of-contract case. However, many contracts—particularly for small amounts—are **oral contracts**, in which the parties spoke about the terms of their agreement but didn't put anything in writing. An oral contract is a valid contract and you can sue if it is breached, but the terms of an oral contract are harder to prove than those of a written one. On the other hand, anything in writing that tends to confirm your version of events will probably be accepted as evidence, particularly if it is signed or was written by the other side.

• **Receipts.** These can be useful proof that a person has been paid.

• **Cancelled checks.** Cancelled checks can provide evidence that you have paid a person, and that he or she has cashed the checks.

• **Expert witnesses.** In most small-claims cases, an expert witness will not be necessary, nor will it be worth the expense. However, you may wish to hire an expert witness in some cases. For example, if you are suing a contractor for poor workmanship, it will be very helpful to have another contractor—preferably one in the same line of work—explain to the judge the problem with the defendant's work. If you had to hire someone to fix the defendant's mistakes, the person who fixed the work would probably make an excellent witness.

• **Letters.** Letters can provide good written evidence of what actually happened—for example, letters to a person who owes you money can be evidence that you asked him or her to repay the debts. However, letters to or from people other than the defendant may or may not be acceptable evidence in your local small-claims court.

Always be sure to have all the evidence you can muster to prove your case. For example, if you are suing a dry cleaner for losing an expensive suit, it is essential that you prove you actually dropped off the suit. A receipt or claim slip from the dry cleaner will be very helpful. If you are suing a contractor for failing to provide adequate services, examples of good evidence would include the repair contract itself, eyewitnesses or an expert witness (such as another contractor), and photographs. When trying to figure out what evidence would be best, ask yourself: If you were the judge, what would you require as proof of your claim?

If you want to submit the evidence of an eyewitness who does not want to come to court, that person may be able to write a letter containing the relevant information. However, not every small-claims court will accept letters or written statements from witnesses. If you can submit a letter from a witness, it should contain the following:

• The date of the statement and location at which it was written
• The name of the court and presiding judge (if you know it)
• The names of the parties and the case number
• The witness's name and occupation
• How, when, where, and what the witness observed—i.e., everything that he or she saw, heard, touched, or smelled that bears upon your case

Check with court personnel in your local small-claims court to find out whether it will accept letters from witnesses. Even if the court does allow letters from witnesses, personal testimony is preferable and should be used whenever possible.

It is a good idea to bring copies of any documentary evidence or photographs for the judge, yourself, and the other party. The judge may have questions about the evidence, and all parties can refer to their copies in order to answer the questions. Having enough copies of your evidence will make it easier on the judge, because you will not have to pass evidence back and forth. Having copies also shows the judge you are prepared and organized, which is always appreciated.

▶ A SAMPLE LETTER FROM AN EYEWITNESS

A letter from a witness might look something like this:

800 Ocean View Lane
San Diego, California

March 31, 2006

Mr. John Smith, Presiding Judge
Small-Claims Court
San Diego, California

Re: Oren Sachar v. Lynn Cohn
Small Claims Case No. 99999

Your Honor:

My name is James Stein. I work as a technician at Superior Sound, which is located in San Diego, California. I am thirty-two years old.

On March 19, 2006, at around 3:00 P.M., I witnessed two movers drop a television while I was inside the residential home located at 7242 Birchcreek, San Diego, California.

I was inside the home with my fiancée and our real estate agent because we were considering making an offer to purchase it. After viewing the dining room, I moved into the living room where two gentlemen were attempting to move a black big-screen television. I was about twenty feet away from them when the television fell, and I was able to see what happened very clearly. The television fell on its screen side, hitting a chair on its way down. No one other than the movers was in the room at the time; my fiancée was upstairs with the real estate agent. I did not get the movers' names, but I do remember that both had dark hair and were wearing blue overalls. I do not recall how tall they were, but neither struck me as very short or very tall. Moments later, when we had left the house and I got into our agent's car, I told her to wait so that I could write down the name written on the side of the truck the movers were using. It was "StudentsMoveU4cheap." I then got the homeowner's number from the agent, and left him a phone message telling him what had happened.

In my understanding, the court case arising from this incident is scheduled for April 18th, 2006. I will be traveling at that time, and will not be able to appear in court.

Sincerely,

James Stein

THE HEARING

On a specified date, you will have to attend a hearing in small-claims court. Small-claims courts are usually much less formal than other state or federal courts. Even so, you should be sure to stand when the judge enters the court, and keep the following tips in mind:

• Be courteous to the judge at all times
• Don't be afraid to ask the judge a question if you don't understand something
• Don't interrupt the other side
• Don't yell, curse, or roll your eyes
• Turn off your cell phone or pager
• Dress appropriately, in order to demonstrate that you respect the court. While a suit isn't necessary in small-claims court, you should dress nicely—as if you were attending church, temple, or mosque.

In a small-claims court hearing, the plaintiff presents his or her case first, followed by the defendant. If you are the plaintiff, you will have a short amount of time in which to explain to the judge what happened to you, what you are seeking from the court, and why you are entitled to it. An effective way of doing this is to begin with what happened. For example, if you are suing a moving company for dropping your television and breaking it, start by telling this to the judge. At this point, don't bother explaining why you were moving out of the house, or when you bought the television and how much it cost. Then tell the judge the amount for which you are suing.

Have all of your physical evidence ready when the judge asks for it. At this point in the proceedings, the judge will probably take a couple of minutes to process your situation and ask you questions (e.g., "How did this happen?" or "How do you know that the defendant dropped your television?"). This will give you the opportunity to tell your story. You should tell your story in a well-organized way that makes it easy for the judge to understand.

Keep in mind that, while you and the opposing party are intimately familiar with your case, the judge is not. Your story might make perfect sense in your head, but if you relate the events out of order, the judge might find it very difficult to follow. A good way to organize your presentation—whether you are the plaintiff or the defendant—is to make a list of the things you want to say, and organize them in the order you want to say them. For each point you plan to make, note any evidence you will use to prove that point. As with any other dispute resolution procedure, the more prepared you are, the better your chances of achieving a favorable outcome.

The plaintiff will present his or her case first. The sidebar below provides some tips on how the plaintiff might prepare and present his or her case.

▶ **AN EXAMPLE OF A PLAINTIFF'S PREPARATION LIST**

In the example of the broken television set, the plaintiff's preparation list might look like this:

- StudentsMoveU4cheap.com dropped my 62-inch television on March 19th, 2006.

- I am asking for $2,345.64 plus court costs because this is what I paid for the television on January 3rd, 2006. The television is totally broken and cannot be repaired. I bought the television at TV Land.

- *Give judge and defendant a copy of the receipt for the television, and the quote from the TV repair shop stating that it would cost more to repair the TV than it is worth.*
- I hired the defendant, StudentsMoveU4cheap, on March 3rd 2006.
  - *Give judge and defendant a copy of the contract I signed when hiring them, and the receipt that proves I paid them.*
- According to the contract, they are responsible for any damage to things they move.
  - *Refer judge and defendant to section 8(b) of the contract I just handed them.*
- I was not at home to see them drop the TV, but I know that it was working in the morning when I left the house, and wasn't working when I got home.
  - *My wife is here to testify to the same thing. (Wife testifies.)*
- I have a witness who saw the movers drop the television. This person was looking at the house as a potential buyer and was in the living room when the TV fell. Unfortunately he couldn't make it to this hearing because he is traveling, but he wrote the following letter.
  - *Hand judge and defendant letter from witness.*
- I also have pictures of the TV after it was moved that show the crack on the outside of the frame.
  - *Show judge and defendant pictures. Tell judge when you took the pictures, and let him know that each one is dated. Show him a receipt that proves when and where the pictures were developed.*
- On March 20th, 2006, I called the owner of the moving company to let her know what happened, at which point she told me she would get back to me.
- The owner called me back on March 31st, 2006, and told me that she spoke with the movers, and that they remember that the television was already broken when they got there.

▶ **AN EXAMPLE OF A DEFENDANT'S PREPARATION LIST**

Assuming the defendant in this example is the owner of the business StudentsMoveU4cheap.com, the defendant's preparation list might look something like this:

- It is true that we moved the plaintiff's television.

- I spoke with the employees (Seth and Brian), who moved the television. They specifically remember the frame being cracked, because Seth cut his hand on it while moving the television.

  - *Seth testifies about the cut on his hand.*

- I know that the plaintiff and his wife said the television was not broken when they left, but they had potential buyers in and out of the house all day. Any one of them could have broken it.

- I am not sure what the witness saw, but maybe it had to do with my employee cutting his hand.

- I felt bad about the television, and that they were not at the house while we were moving, so I offered to give them a $100 discount.

- We are pretty good at what we do, and that is why we have been in business eighteen years with no complaints.

  - *Hand judge and plaintiff copy of business review published in San Diego Times.*

After the plaintiff has spoken, the defendant has a chance to present his or her version of events. If you are the defendant, you will have read the complaint, and will probably have a pretty good idea of what the plaintiff will say and what evidence the plaintiff will present. There are often surprises, however, so you need to be flexible. The above sidebar provides some tips on how the defendant might prepare and present his or her case.

APPEALS

Whenever you go to court, there is always a chance that the judge will rule against you and that you won't achieve the result you wanted. Small-claims court is no exception. After both sides present their cases, the judge will make a decision and rule accordingly. Most states allow the losing side to appeal or challenge the judge's decision. An appeal must be filed within a certain period of time, usually between ten and thirty days after the decision has been made.

In some states, such as California, an appeal will automatically result in a new trial, sometimes called a **trial de novo**. In this type of trial, the court will hear the case without regard to what happened at the first hearing. The parties start over from scratch. For example, suppose Brenda and Shanterria go to small-claims court in California over a dispute about a used car that Brenda sold to Shanterria. Shanterria insists that Brenda

---

⚠️ DEFEND YOURSELF!

Sometimes defendants don't want to show up at court; they think that if they don't go, nothing can happen to them. But nothing could be further from the truth. Failure to appear in court will almost certainly result in a **default judgment** against the defendant for the full amount sought by the plaintiff, plus court costs. This means that the plaintiff wins her or his case without having to argue it or even produce evidence.

Even if you are sure that you'll lose your case, it is still worth going to court so that the plaintiff has to present his or her case. Perhaps the plaintiff will not have sufficient evidence to convince the judge that he or she should win. If you don't go to court, you will lose the opportunity to ask for court orders that may help you. If you lose in some states, for example, you can ask the judge to let you make payments in installments. This alone can be a good reason to show up.

sold her a lemon, and that Brenda should pay the cost of repairs in accordance with the state's lemon law. Brenda claims that Shanterria's failure to properly operate the stick shift caused damage to the car. In addition, Brenda argues that the state's lemon law does not apply, because she sold the car before the law took effect. The judge rules in Shanterria's favor and orders Brenda to refund Shanterria's money. In California, cases may be appealed over issues of fact (as opposed to issues of law), so Brenda can appeal on the grounds that the judge made the wrong decision about who damaged the car.

In other states, however, a court may not reconsider the facts of your case in an appeal; instead, an appeal may arise only from an allegation that the judge made a legal mistake. In such a state, Brenda would be unable to appeal on the grounds that the small-claims-court judge made the wrong decision about who damaged the car. The judge's decision on that issue would be final. Instead, Brenda could only base an appeal on the issue of whether the state's lemon law applies to her case. This is not an issue relating to the individual facts of the case; rather, it is an issue relating to the way in which the law *applies* to those facts.

If you lose your case in small-claims court and think you may have grounds for appeal, talk with the small-claims clerk to find out what rules apply to appeals in your jurisdiction.

In most states, you are entitled to have a lawyer represent you in your appeal. However, small-claims appeals sometimes are handled separately from regular cases, and often use the same relaxed procedures as the original hearings. If you are in a state that handles appeals in this manner, you might consider representing yourself and proceeding without a lawyer for the

(i) JURY APPEALS

A few states permit jury trials on appeal, but most states don't. To find out the rules in your state, talk to the clerk at your small-claims court.

same reasons you chose small-claims court initially. If you intend to represent yourself in an appeal, go to the courthouse prior to your court date and observe a few small-claims appeals to develop an idea of how they are handled.

COLLECTING AN AWARD

If you are the plaintiff, winning a case usually means that you are entitled to the amount of money you were seeking from the defendant. If you win a case in small-claims court, the judge usually will issue a decision stating that you won, and ordering the defendant to pay you a sum of money. Surprisingly, the decision alone is enough to satisfy some plaintiffs—even if they don't

( ) TALKING TO A LAWYER

Q. If I go to small-claims court and I am not happy with the result, couldn't I mediate or negotiate the settlement later? Is it a good idea to start in small-claims court and negotiate or mediate if I lose?

A. In most states, the decision of a small-claims court is final and binding if no one appeals within a specified period of time, usually about thirty days. If you lose in small-claims court and don't appeal, or don't even have the right to appeal, you will probably be in a very weak position for purposes of mediating or negotiating any further. In order to preserve any hope of winning your case, you will probably have to file an appeal as a protective measure.

Remember: It is not a good idea to start in small-claims court. Try to negotiate or mediate first, and then go to court—even small-claims court—only if you cannot resolve the dispute any other way.

—Answer by Judge Robert Shenkin,
Court of Common Pleas of Chester County,
West Chester, Pennsylvania

collect a cent of the judgment. Some people simply want to hear a judge say that they are right, and the defendant is wrong.

However, most people want to receive the money they are owed. If a judge rules in your favor and the defendant is a business or person of substance (i.e., a person of good character) with roots in the community, you will probably be paid without difficulty. Unfortunately, however, it may take additional effort to collect money from some defendants.

After ruling on your case, the judge might create a payment schedule, but will not participate in the collection process. Every court has its own procedures for collecting on a judgment. If you don't get paid, you might be able to get an order requiring the defendant's employer to pay some of the defendant's wages directly to you. Or, if you can locate the defendant's bank account, you might be able to get an order directing the bank to pay you the amount you are owed from that account. Or perhaps you can require the defendant to disclose his or her income or assets in response to a series of written questions (sometimes called **interrogatories in aid of execution**) or in a question-and-answer session under oath (called a **deposition**). But if the defendant doesn't pay you voluntarily, collecting on your judgment will require you to make more filings and expend even more effort.

THE WORLD AT YOUR FINGERTIPS

• For a comprehensive guide to small-claims courts, including links to information about small-claims courts in every state, visit *www.consumeraffairs.com/consumerism/small_states.htm*.

• Nolo.com, one of the leading publishers of legal self-help titles and articles, has published *Everybody's Guide to Small Claims Court*, which provides more detailed information about small-claims court procedures, and tips for representing yourself in small-claims court. The book is available from the Nolo.com website, *www.nolo.com*.

• Remember: Small-claims courts procedures are different in every state. However, some states' websites do provide useful general information. Visit the website of the Virginia state courts at *www.courts.state.va.us/pamphlets/small_claims.html* for some straightforward information about small-claims courts procedures in that state. In addition, the Connecticut courts website at *www.jud2.state.ct.us/Small_Claims/* includes answers to many questions about that state's procedures, as well as links to sample forms.

REMEMBER THIS

• Small-claims courts are also known as "magistrate's courts" and "county courts." All small-claims courts impose caps on the amount of money that can be sought in any case.

• Small-claims court can provide a low-cost alternative to litigation in a public setting. You can participate in small-claims court without a lawyer, and your case can be resolved relatively quickly.

• Small-claims courts are regulated by the states. It is important that you get information specific to your small-claims court from your local courthouse.

• Before you sue someone in small-claims court, make sure that litigation is the best way to resolve your issue—and not negotiation, mediation, or arbitration.

CHAPTER 6

Court Procedures
in Civil Cases

Understanding a Trial from Start to Finish

The judge cleared her throat and spoke:"Opening statements in *Petersen Corporation v. Chagas Incorporated* will now begin." Cleo Chagas, CEO of Chagas Incorporated, sat quietly and looked at the jury. She thought to herself, "These twelve strangers will decide whether my business will have to pay Petersen Corporation $420,000 for a deal that no one intended would go sour . . . My career and reputation are in their hands." Cleo was nervous. She was confident that the facts and law were in her favor, but she was unsure if the jury would see it the same way.

Six days later, the jury returned a verdict for Chagas Incorporated. Cleo was thrilled that her company had won. Her employees were relieved, and her customers were happy. Her professional reputation was saved. However, Cleo also took a moment to reflect on what the lawsuit had cost. The company had been involved in the suit for four years, and had spent substantial amounts on legal fees. The litigation had also ensured that Chagas would never work with Petersen Corporation again.

Litigation is a formal, public process for resolving disputes, in which one party files a lawsuit against another, and a judge or jury hears the case in court and issues a binding decision. Resolving a dispute by means of a lawsuit offers the litigants an opportunity to change the law, and to create legal precedents for similar cases that follow. However, litigation can be a time-consuming and expensive process—one in which there are

(i) A GLIMPSE INTO THE COURTHOUSE

The courthouse may seem intimidating. The perception of most new-comers is that a visit to court will be unpleasant. However, some famil-iarity with the courthouse may put you more at ease.

Often the first people you will see in a courthouse are armed officers near the front entrance. The officers may be court marshals, bailiffs, or security personnel. The court staff are usually friendly and will provide you with directions and information. To ensure everyone's safety, most courtrooms now have metal detectors. As an additional security mea-sure, most courts today require that every person entering the court-house show personal identification, such as a driver's license, state identification card, or passport.

Once inside the court building, you will be directed to the office of the court clerk. This is the main filing and information center of the court-house. This is where your lawyer will file all papers and pay all fees re-lating to your litigation. The clerk's office can also provide you with judges' schedules and information about local rules specific to that courthouse.

For purposes of your case, the most important place in the courthouse is the courtroom. The courtroom is where the judge hears all court pro-ceedings, from preliminary matters to the trial. You will probably recog-nize the judge's bench, the jury box, and the two tables for the plaintiff and defendant. Behind the tables is a space for members of the public, or for litigants to wait until their cases are called. A court reporter will be present in the courtroom to record and transcribe the court proceedings. Next to the judge you will see the judge's clerk, who keeps track of the evidence in each case. Once court is in session, this area is not accessi-ble to persons in the courtroom.

It is important to remember that, whenever you are in the presence of a judge, you and your case are being evaluated. As a sign of respect, it is customary to stand whenever the judge enters or leaves the courtroom.

winners, losers, and parties like Cleo, who feel like they win and lose on the same day.

Courts, with their technical language and formal procedures, can be confusing and intimidating to the average person—and even to some lawyers. In this country, we really have fifty-one different court systems: one for each state, and a federal system. And although the systems have many similarities, they also differ legally and procedurally in ways too numerous to explain thoroughly in this chapter. Rather than provide details of each individual court system, this chapter will provide a general outline of court procedures. If you are involved in a lawsuit, talk to your lawyer about the specific procedures that apply in your state.

CIVIL AND CRIMINAL CASES

In the United States, there are two separate types of cases: criminal and civil. **Criminal cases** involve violations of criminal laws. In criminal cases, the court seeks to deter crime and punish guilty parties by imposing sentences, which include fines payable to the government, confinement in jail, and probation. In criminal cases the county, state, or local government prosecutor brings the lawsuit on behalf of the public, or **the people**. The prosecutor's responsibility is to present the facts to the judge or jury. In a criminal case, if you lose, you are found **guilty**. Because liberty may be at stake, criminal defendants have important rights, including the right to a jury trial, the right to be represented by a lawyer, and the right (under the Fifth Amendment of the Constitution) to not give evidence that may be self-incriminating.

In **civil cases**, one party generally seeks money from the other party as compensation for a loss he or she has suffered. Or one party could seek an **injunction**, which is a court order mandating action. The case is decided when a judge or jury makes a decision in favor of one party. In a civil case, if you lose the lawsuit you may be found **liable,** which means you are responsible for paying money to the winning party and complying with any other court orders. A civil judge or jury cannot punish a liable party with jail time.

Cases involving divorce, child custody, and probate are civil cases. Some civil disputes arise out of situations that involve criminal actions. For example, if Rick, a drunk driver in Atlanta, crashes into Carolyn's car and damages her property, Rick can face two lawsuits. The county prosecutor will charge Rick for driving while intoxicated and seek criminal sanctions such as revocation of his driver's license, a hefty fine, and possibly even jail time. Carolyn can seek money damages to replace her car in a separate civil suit.

In many states, there are separate courts to hear civil and criminal cases. In some states, there is just one court that hears both civil and criminal cases. This chapter will focus solely on civil cases.

THE O. J. LESSON

For most Americans, one case that especially highlighted the differences between criminal and civil courts was the O. J. Simpson case. In a criminal court, O. J. was found not guilty of murder. But in the civil case, he was found liable for the deaths of his ex-wife, Nicole Brown Simpson, and her friend, Ron Goldman. The civil court ordered O. J. to pay a large sum of money to the victims' families.

The reason the case ended differently in the two courts is that criminal courts and civil courts require different **standards of proof**. In order to find someone guilty in criminal court, the judge or jury must believe that the evidence proves the person's guilt **beyond a reasonable doubt**. In civil courts, the judge or jury must be convinced of the person's liability **by a preponderance of the evidence**. This means that it is easier to prove liability in a civil case than to prove guilt in a criminal case.

THE PARTIES TO LITIGATION

The person, group of people, or companies involved in a civil case are called the **parties**. The party that commences the case is called the **plaintiff**. The party that is being sued is called the **defendant**. In some courts, such as in family courts, the person who files the suit is called the **petitioner** and the person against whom the case is filed is called the **respondent**.

Litigate is simply a legal term that means "engage in legal proceedings." A civil dispute in the courts is often said to be **in litigation**. A lawyer who appears in court in connection with a contested case is called a **litigator**.

TYPICAL CIVIL COURT CASES

A broad array of cases may be heard in civil court. Typical civil cases include contract or business disputes, and cases in which one individual sues another. For example, civil courts might hear cases in which:

• A former employee sues a company over dangerous working conditions, wrongful termination, pension issues, or injuries

• A consumer brings a lawsuit against a company because he was injured by one of the company's products

• One small business sues another claiming infringement of a patent

Common family law cases include:

• Child custody and support disputes, in which parents cannot agree who should have custody of their child

• Alimony cases, in which a person seeks alimony from a former spouse

Common wills and estates disputes include:

• Disputes arising from a will, as when a parent has cut a child out of a will

• Disputes arising during probate, as when one family member seems to be trying to get all of the deceased person's most valuable assets

Common personal-injury disputes include:

• Cases in which a person is injured as a result of another person's negligence in a store or other public place

• Disputes involving injuries arising from car accidents

• Medical malpractice cases, in which a person claims he or she has been injured as a result of negligence by a doctor

IS LITIGATION RIGHT FOR YOU?

In the heat of the moment, it is easy to say "I'll see you in court!" But the decision to file a lawsuit should only be made after serious deliberation. This section outlines some of the questions you should ask yourself before you initiate a lawsuit.

Do You Have a Case?

Before bringing suit, you must determine whether you have a case. It might be unpleasant when your neighbor uses a jackhammer in his driveway at 6 A.M., but if a city ordinance allows him to do so, you don't have grounds for a lawsuit.

⚠ THE COURT DOESN'T APPRECIATE FRIVOLITY

Baseless litigation wastes time and money. Courts will punish parties and/or lawyers who file claims simply to harass someone, waste time, or advance any other inappropriate or frivolous motive. The most common punishment for such behavior is dismissal of the case, and an order for the party and/or attorney to pay the other side's legal fees. Such sanctions are imposed only when a case has absolutely no merit.

To determine whether you have a case and whether you should file a lawsuit, consult with a lawyer. Your lawyer will ask you to explain the nature of your dispute, and will try to determine whether

1. you had a legal right;
2. that legal right was violated by another person; and
3. that violation led to damages that can be remedied with money.

If you can answer these threshold questions in the affirmative, you may have a case—also called a **cause of action**.

Do You Have the Evidence You Need?

Evidence is essential. If you anticipate any kind of legal dispute, keep as potential evidence any relevant receipts, letters, e-mails, credit card statements, cancelled checks, and quotes for repairs. Take pictures. Write down the names of witnesses, license plate numbers, and driver's license numbers. And in the event of an accident, always request that a police officer write up a report. As an example, if a car slams into you while you are riding your new Harley-Davidson motorcycle, important evidence in a lawsuit might include a police report, a detailed doctor's report, documentation of any lost wages, and quotes from mechanics regarding the cost of repairing damage to your motorcycle.

In your first consultation with your lawyer, his or her assessment of whether you have a case will depend in part on the strength of your evidence.

▶ **A LAWYER IS BOUND BY A CODE OF ETHICS**

Lawyers swear a duty to the court. This means that lawyers cannot knowingly lie in court. If a lawyer knows that you are lying, he or she may be forced to resign from your case.

Are You Filing On Time?

When filing a lawsuit, perhaps the most important factor to keep in mind is the statute of limitations. A **statute of limitations** is a law establishing a time limit within which parties must take steps to enforce their rights. This means that, after an incident takes place, you have a limited amount of time to sue someone in connection with that incident. If you don't file your lawsuit before the deadline, your lawsuit will be **time-barred**. This means that you will never be able to file, no matter how strong your case.

Why are there time limits on filing a case? The answer is that, over time, the value of evidence diminishes—witnesses forget what they saw, documents get lost, and so forth. As time passes, it becomes more difficult for a judge or jury to determine the facts of a case. Time limits thus promote efficiency and accuracy in the courts.

The statute of limitations usually begins to "run"—that is, the clock usually starts ticking—immediately after the incident giving rise to your dispute. For example, if Mario runs his SUV into Roberta's Volkswagen Beetle, Roberta has two years from the date of the accident in which to file a lawsuit. This is because the statute of limitations for automotive accidents is two years in her state.

However, sometimes the statute-of-limitations clock does not begin to run until an injury is discovered. For example, if you were exposed to a harmful substance while working in a factory in the early 1990s, but did not learn until 2006 that the substance was cancer-causing, the statute-of-limitations clock would not begin to run until 2006. If the statute of limitations in your state is two years, you would have until 2008 to file your lawsuit.

Different states have different filing deadlines, and different kinds of cases have different statutes of limitations. For example, the statute of limitations in personal-injury cases is usually one to two years, but the limitation period for breach of a written contract is usually between three and eight years. Most statutes of limitations allow plaintiffs at least one year from the moment of

(i) WHEN THE CLOCK STARTS TO RUN

In the 1920s, a doctor performed an operation on a woman, carelessly leaving a surgical sponge in her abdomen. This sponge remained in the patient's body for two-and-a-half years, by which time it seemed that the statute of limitations—which presumably began to run on the date the sponge was left inside the patient—had expired. However, the patient was still able to sue successfully for medical malpractice. In this case, the court held that the statute of limitations had begun to run only when the injury itself was complete—that is, when the sponge was finally removed.

---

injury to file a lawsuit. However, time limits vary greatly, and laws can change. If you think you may have a case, consult with a lawyer quickly to find out when your filing deadline will expire. If the statute of limitations expires before you file your complaint, there is rarely anything a lawyer or judge can do to help you.

Can Litigation Provide the Solution You Want?

If you win a civil case, the court can issue several kinds of orders to enforce your rights or redress wrongdoing. These orders are called **remedies**.

In most civil cases, the appropriate remedy is an order for the defendant to pay money, called **damages**. There are several types of damages. **Compensatory damages** are the most common type of damages awarded by a court. As the name suggests, compensatory damages are monies paid to an injured party to compensate the person for losses he or she sustained as a direct result of an injury. The court will award the amount of money required to return an injured person to the position he or she enjoyed prior to the injury. Compensatory damages are often awarded in personal-injury and breach-of-contract cases.

The court may also award **punitive damages** if there is evidence of fraud or malicious conduct on the part of the losing party. Punitive damages are intended to punish the losing party, and discourage others from engaging in similar behavior. **Nominal damages** are small amounts of damages awarded to a party who wins a case, but is unable to prove that he or she sustained significant damages.

When deciding whether to file a lawsuit, an important consideration is whether the person or company you intend to sue has the money or resources to pay you if you win. If the person you want to sue is bankrupt or has very few resources, he or she may be **judgment-proof**. This means that even if you win the case, the person will not be able to pay you. Sometimes another person, a business, or an insurance company may also be responsible for your loss. Talk to your lawyer about whether you may have a cause of action against a party that is better able to compensate you for your loss—a party other than the person who directly caused your loss or injury.

Civil courts can also issue orders that prohibit a party from doing something. These orders are called **injunctions**. For example, a person might seek an injunction to prevent a chemical company from releasing chemicals into a local river. Or a person might seek an injunction to prevent a neighbor from cutting down trees along a shared property line. Occasionally a court will issue an order to compel someone to do something. This kind of order is called a **mandatory injunction**.

In some contract cases, monetary damages may not adequately compensate the plaintiff. In such cases, courts can also make orders for **specific performance**. An order for specific performance requires the person who breached the contract to perform the contract as originally agreed. When possible, however, courts prefer to award monetary damages.

If you are considering a lawsuit, think about whether a court will be able to provide the kind of remedy you want. A lawsuit may be an excellent course of action if you are seeking money, trying to prevent someone from doing something, or trying to compel someone to do something. However, a lawsuit may be inappropriate if you want a more creative solution.

(i) THE TOLL ON DEFENDANTS

Litigation can be particularly hard on defendants. The mere accusation of wrongdoing can permanently tarnish a defendant's reputation. After all, would you leave your children at a day care center that had been slapped with allegations of physical abuse, even if you knew that the case had been dropped? What if you knew the day care center had won the case in court?

How Will Litigation Affect You?

When deciding whether to file a lawsuit, you should consider the short- and long-term effects that a lawsuit might have on your personal life. Sometimes lawsuits cause people on both sides of a case to become unhealthily obsessed with their legal situations. Lawsuits can also be time-consuming and expensive, and public disclosure of one's private affairs can be stressful and unforgiving for both plaintiffs and defendants.

A lawsuit can be divisive for an office, a business, a community, a friendship, or even a family. Many personal and business relationships cannot survive a lawsuit. Healthy family and business relationships are valuable to most people, and the risk of potential damage to these relationships should be something you consider when deciding whether to negotiate, mediate, arbitrate, litigate, or walk away and take a loss.

Is Precedent Important?

Unlike any other dispute resolution mechanism, a lawsuit creates a binding legal **precedent**. This means that the decision in your case will help determine the outcome of future cases. Legal precedent is what allows courts to be a vehicle for social change. For example, in 1954, the Supreme Court held in *Brown v. Board of Education* that it was unlawful for public schools to be segregated by race. This decision affected not only the plaintiff's school in Topeka, Kansas, but every public school in the United States.

Most lawsuits will not make it to the U.S. Supreme Court, but the interpretation of the law in your case may affect other cases in your jurisdiction. Thus, for example, if a company exposes numerous employees to asbestos, and a lawsuit is filed against it, the resolution of that lawsuit may affect the outcome of numerous other asbestos-related lawsuits. If a court finds the company liable, it is likely to face more lawsuits—and other companies in similar situations are also likely to face lawsuits. If the company is not held liable, similar types of lawsuits might taper off, or completely cease to be filed. Similarly, if you are an employee who has been exposed to lead poisoning, you would likely pay close attention to the outcome of an asbestos-related case. Even if the circumstances of your case were not identical to those of an asbestos case, they might be similar—and the legal reasoning used to decide the asbestos case might be similar to the reasoning that would be used to decide yours. The outcome of the case, and the reasoning behind it, might affect—and help you to predict—the outcome of your own case.

As these examples illustrate, the fact that a case will set a legal precedent may constitute an advantage or disadvantage of litigation, depending on your circumstances.

Have You Exhausted Your Administrative Options?

If your case involves enforcement of state or federal laws, then you may not be permitted to file a lawsuit until you have sought redress through the procedures of an administrative agency. Administrative agencies are government bodies that act to enforce laws. For example, the National Labor Relations Board enforces the National Labor Relations Act, and the Equal Employment Opportunity Commission enforces several laws that prohibit discrimination at work.

You can initiate a case with an administrative agency by filing a **complaint**, in which you give information about what happened and why you think it was unlawful. For example, if you were discriminated against at work because you're female, then in your complaint you would need to describe the circumstances that gave rise to the discrimination you allege, give details of any evidence or witnesses, and state your belief that the law was broken. Some agencies have complaint forms available on their websites where you can submit your complaint directly. Others prefer if you mail in your information and evidence. There are specific time limits for making a complaint.

Once a complaint is submitted, the agency will determine whether the case has merit. This process may take time—many administrative agencies have long backlogs of complaints. The agency may decide to dismiss the case, or it may conduct further investigation. It may decide to refer the case to mediation, or refer it directly to an Administrative Law Judge (ALJ), who will hear evidence about the dispute from the parties (all of whom are usually represented by lawyers), and make a decision. Should either side wish to appeal, the decision is generally reviewable by a panel of ALJs. Further appeals may go to a U.S. Court of Appeals.

When an administrative agency completes its investigation, it will send a letter to the parties, which will state whether it found reasonable cause to believe the law was violated. This is called a **right-to-sue** letter. Once you receive this letter, you have the right to file a lawsuit in state or federal court within a certain time period. You may file a lawsuit even if the agency decided that the law was not violated (although such a decision should probably give you pause to consider whether your case is strong enough to win a lawsuit).

INITIATING A LAWSUIT

If you have a cause of action, the statute of limitations has not expired, you know that litigation will provide the remedy you want, and you've exhausted your administrative options, you may

⚠️ **HURDLES TO FILING A LAWSUIT**

There are many other reasons you may not be able to file a lawsuit, even if you wish to do so. For example, you may not be able to file a lawsuit if you have signed a mandatory arbitration clause in a contract. As discussed in chapter 5, such clauses dictate that your dispute must be resolved by arbitration. Furthermore, depending on the specific rules of the arbitration or grievance procedure in which you have participated, a court may not be able to hear any appeal.

You may also have problems filing a lawsuit if you have not yet exhausted all other avenues of appeal. Many employers, hospitals, health insurers, and housing administrations have internal grievance procedures, similar to the administrative procedures described above, that you must exhaust before filing a lawsuit.

---

decide to proceed with a lawsuit. Before you can get to court, however, there are several important things you must do. For starters, you must decide whom and where to sue.

Finding the Defendant

Before you can initiate a lawsuit, you must identify and locate the right person to sue. While this might sound obvious, the identity of the person at fault is not always obvious. For example, if you are walking down the street and break your ankle stepping into a pothole, you will have to answer several questions before you decide whom to sue. Who owns the property? Is it government property or private property? Who is responsible for the maintenance? Or suppose you receive negligent treatment at a hospital. Should you sue the doctor or the hospital, or both? Imagine you suspect that contaminated drinking water at a local school could be responsible for an unusually high number of brain tumors in local children. Upon investigation, you learn that two chemical companies with a history of illegal dumping have factories located along the same river as the school. You may not know which company to sue. If high levels of radon in the school's first-floor classrooms may also be contributing to the incidence of cancer, you may have even more possible defendants.

Fortunately, courts allow you to initiate a lawsuit against multiple defendants. You may then work out who is at fault during the discovery process (discussed later in this chapter). Or perhaps several parties will be liable, and you can seek to recover damages from all of them.

Jurisdiction

Once you know whom to sue, you must decide whether to file suit in state court or federal court. Each court system has different jurisdiction. **Jurisdiction** is a court's right or authority to apply the law.

State courts handle the vast majority of cases. This is because state laws govern the great bulk of legal business—traffic offenses, divorce, wills and estates, and the buying and selling of property. State courts are located in many towns and almost all counties. These are the courts with which most of us are likely to come into contact.

Forty-five states have two or more levels of state trial courts. **Special jurisdiction courts** have jurisdiction limited to specific types of cases (they usually hear relatively minor disputes), and are typically dominated by traffic cases. **General jurisdiction courts** hear the more serious cases, and are sometimes subdivided by subject area.

Federal courts are generally more formal than state courts, and the dollar amounts in dispute tend to be higher. Federal courts deal with matters of federal law such as civil rights, employee benefits, and bankruptcy.

Your lawyer will help you determine which court has jurisdiction over your case.

( ) TALKING TO A LAWYER

Q. Are there situations in which I can choose whether to file in state court or federal court? If so, which one is more beneficial for me as a plaintiff?

A. Consult a lawyer, and let him or her decide. If your case is significant enough to file in a regular trial court, you would be making a big mistake if you tried to handle the case on your own. Choosing the proper court is a decision too complex for a nonlawyer to make alone.

—Answer by Judge Robert Shenkin,
Court of Common Pleas of Chester County,
West Chester, Pennsylvania

PRETRIAL PROCEDURES

Once you've determined whom to sue and where to sue them, you can file a lawsuit. You will have to take many formal steps in order to file a case and prepare for trial. Your lawyer will take the lead in preparing all the documents described in this section. If you know what goes into each document, and its purpose, you will be able to assist your lawyer in putting together the best possible case.

Filing the Complaint

In most jurisdictions, a lawsuit begins when the plaintiff files a **complaint** in the proper court. The complaint notifies the court and the defendant about the subject matter of the lawsuit. In most state courts and in the federal courts, the complaint must show the existence of a legal right and claim that there has been a violation of that legal right. Remember: The complaint must be filed before the statute of limitations expires.

The contents of the complaint can vary from state to state. In most states, the complaint contains five pieces of information:

1. The identities of the parties: Who is suing whom?

2. The jurisdictional statement: Why is this court the right court?

3. The underlying facts leading to the litigation: What happened?

4. The legal claims: What laws were broken?

5. The damages sought (also called **claim of relief**): What is the plaintiff asking the judge or jury to award?

The complaint must accurately identify the parties. It must include the parties' addresses and a brief statement about their relevance to the lawsuit. For example, if you were suing a man who sold you a cracked surfboard that caused you severe injuries, you would list in your complaint his name, address, and role in the lawsuit (e.g., that he is the "owner, operator and salesperson of Jack's Surf Shop in Huntington Beach, California"). As the plaintiff, you would provide your own name, address, and role in the lawsuit (e.g., that you are the "purchaser of the defective surfboard from Jack's Surf Shop").

Your complaint must also include a jurisdictional statement explaining why you are filing a lawsuit in this particular court. In the surfboard example, you would state that you are filing in California because the defendant is a resident of California, or because the defendant does a considerable amount of business in California, or because the events leading to the litigation took place in California.

The complaint must also include a brief summary of the events giving rise to the lawsuit. This summary must be sufficiently detailed for the defendant to understand what the suit is about. For example, in a case arising from an auto accident, a sufficiently detailed summary might read as follows: "the defendant, Elena Cohn, owner and driver of a blue Chevrolet Suburban, drove her sport-utility vehicle into the plaintiff's Toyota

Corolla on the morning of July 5, 2006, at the corner of Michigan Avenue and Chicago Avenue."

A complaint should also include information about what law was broken, or why the plaintiff is entitled to relief. In the above example, a statement that "damage was caused as a result of the defendant's negligence" would probably be sufficient.

Lastly, the complaint should include a statement about the remedy the plaintiff is seeking. This is sometimes called the plaintiff's **prayer for relief**. Some courts require plaintiffs to break down their desired remedy into categories of damages (i.e., $30,000 in compensatory damages and $150,000 in punitive damages, for a total of $180,000 in damages).

When you file a complaint with the court, you must also arrange for the defendant to be issued a summons. A **summons** is simply a legal notice informing the defendant that a complaint has been filed, and providing the defendant with the date of the first hearing and the location of the court.

Service of Process

The complaint and summons must be given to the defendant through a special form of delivery called **service of process**. In most jurisdictions, service requires copies of the documents to be personally delivered (**served**) to the defendant at his or her home, or given to a person who resides at the defendant's house who is at least eighteen years of age. Documents must be served within a certain period of time after the complaint is filed. Usually courts will not allow a plaintiff to serve process for his or her own lawsuit. Service is usually carried out by a law enforcement agent, such as a sheriff or bailiff of the court, or through a private process server. Process servers generally charge a fee for this service.

The reason there are strict rules about service is that defendants have a fundamental right to defend themselves. The service rules are designed to ensure that the defendant receives fair and timely notice of the lawsuit he or she faces.

▶ **THE FORMAT OF A COMPLAINT**

The information in a complaint usually is organized into a list. Each fact or legal assertion is individually numbered and stands alone as a single paragraph, called a **claim** or **count**. For example, a typical complaint might read as follows:

1. Elena Cohn is a resident of Chicago, Illinois.

2. Elena Cohn owns a blue Chevrolet Suburban.

3. On the morning of July 5, 2006, Elena Cohn was driving her Suburban.

4. On the morning of July 5, 2006, Elena Cohn ran a red light heading eastbound on Chicago Avenue at the intersection with Michigan Avenue.

5. Following and as a result of running the red light, Ms. Cohn collided with plaintiff's Toyota Corolla.

6. Plaintiff sustained $7,200 in car repair costs, $2,350 damages in medical expenses, and $1,275 in lost wages from work.

This format enables the defendant to agree or disagree with each numbered paragraph in his or her answer to the complaint. This will allow the court to see where the disagreement between the parties really lies. Thus, the defendant in this example might agree to paragraphs one through three, but deny paragraphs four through six. If Ms. Cohn has never been to Chicago and has never been inside a Chevrolet Suburban, she could deny all six paragraphs.

Filing the Answer

An **answer** is a defendant's response to a complaint. Usually the defendant has approximately thirty days after being served with a complaint to file an answer with the court.

In the answer, the defendant can deny the entire complaint, deny particular portions of the complaint, agree to parts of the

ⓘ DEFAULT JUDGMENT

If you have properly served the defendant with a complaint and summons, but the defendant does not file an answer within the required time period, you can ask the court to enter a **default judgment** against the defendant. Entry of a default judgment means that the defendant loses the case. The court assumes that the defendant is not contesting anything in the complaint, and issues an order granting the plaintiff everything for which he or she has asked.

If the defendant subsequently tells the court that he or she had a good reason for not responding to the complaint, the court may vacate the default judgment and give the defendant a chance to mount a defense.

---

complaint, state that he or she does not have enough information to respond to the complaint, raise defenses, and even state a counterclaim against the plaintiff. If the defendant does not deny or object to a claim, the court will assume the defendant agrees to the claim. Agreements to parts of the complaint are called **admissions**.

For example, suppose a complaint reads as follows:

1. Plaintiff rents an apartment from defendant located in Boston, Massachusetts.

2. Plaintiff's diamond watch was located at the residence rented from defendant.

3. As landlord, the defendant has keys to the plaintiff's property.

4. On January 22nd, the defendant entered the plaintiff's property and stole a diamond watch worth $37,000.

The defendant's response could read:

1. As for claim 1 asserted in plaintiff's complaint: Admitted

2. As for claim 2 asserted in plaintiff's complaint: Defendant does not have enough information to deny or admit this statement at this time.

3. As for claim 3 asserted in plaintiff's complaint: Admitted

4. As for claim 4 asserted in plaintiff's complaint: Denied

5. The defendant was in Juneau, Alaska from January 20th to February 3rd on a Royal Norwegian cruise.

6. Defendant has observed numerous guests enter and leave plaintiff's aparment.

7. Plaintiff has spread false rumors concerning the theft of the watch to the defendant's detriment, and therefore the defendant wishes to make a counterclaim of slander against plaintiff.

In this example, the answer not only addresses each and every specific claim in the complaint, but also states facts that can be used in defense to the claim, and asserts a counterclaim.

Discovery

Discovery is a fact-finding process. Each party asks the other side for information, and asks questions of the other side's witnesses. The purpose of discovery is to collect evidence for your case and evaluate the strength of the other party's case. The more each party knows about the other side's case, the more likely it is to realize the weaknesses of its own case and have an incentive to settle. Discovery may involve reading and reviewing thousands of documents, and interviewing dozens of witnesses. It takes lawyers a lot of time, and can become very expensive. Parties often quarrel about what information they need to provide, adding to the delay and expense of litigation.

The important point for you to understand about discovery is that your private information may be up for grabs. The lawyer for the other side may have the right to read your private correspondence—including what you may have thought were private e-mails—and ask you invasive questions.

One of the most common tools used in discovery is the deposition. **Depositions** are out-of-court statements provided under oath to the lawyer for the other party. In a deposition, what you say is transcribed, recorded, or videotaped. Most people do not like depositions because they entail questions from another person's lawyer, who hopes to uncover information that will strengthen his or her case. Your lawyer is generally present as well,

(i) THE PRIVILEGE EXCEPTION

The American legal system values confidentiality between you and your lawyer. Accordingly, what you say or write to your lawyer concerning your legal case is protected by **attorney-client privilege**, and is not subject to discovery.

A lawyer can't waive attorney-client privilege on your behalf. However, if *you* share privileged material with someone else—like the local bartender or your hairdresser—then you may lose the protection of privilege.

and the lawyers may have heated disagreements, which makes many people nervous and/or confused. A court reporter recording the entire conversation verbatim can also add to the pressure. Moreover, the questions asked can be very personal, and the parties generally must answer any questions they are asked.

Pretrial and Settlement Conferences

After the other side files an answer to your complaint, the judge will schedule a pretrial conference. The **pretrial conference** is an opportunity for the judge and parties to discuss the issues, plan discovery, and schedule dates for mediation and trial.

The judge will have a sense of where the parties disagree and will be able to determine whether there is a genuine dispute that warrants taking the case to trial. If the judge thinks the case is ripe for settlement, he or she may schedule a **settlement conference** to explore settlement options. A settlement conference usually takes a few hours and is led by a magistrate judge who is not directly involved in the case. At the conference, the magistrate judge might apply some indirect or direct pressure on the parties to reach a compromise and resolve their differences. The magistrate judge in a settlement conference will evaluate the weaknesses of each party's case in private, not in the presence of the opposing party. If the case does not settle, it goes back to the

( ) TALKING TO A LAWYER

Q. *What kinds of sanctions can be imposed on lawyers and clients who fail to comply with reasonable discovery requests?*

A. If a lawyer or party does not provide reasonable discovery, the court may require the party or lawyer to pay the other side's attorney's fees and any costs incurred to obtain the information. If no other sanctions are appropriate, the court can also strike (or remove) the party's pleadings or dismiss the case.

—Answer by Judge Goldstein,
Law Offices of Alvin H. Goldstein Jr.,
San Rafael, California

---

trial judge who then continues with the motions and discovery, or begins the trial. While many judges utilize another judge or magistrate judge to conduct these talks, some judges hold settlement conferences for their own cases. This is a controversial practice within the judiciary.

There are several differences between settlement conferences and mediation. Settlement conferences tend to be shorter, and more focused on the strengths and weaknesses of the parties' cases. A mediation, on the other hand, allows the parties to discuss their needs and interests and explore creative solutions for resolving their dispute.

THE TRIAL

If a case is not settled, it will go to trial. The **trial** is a formal hearing at which both sides present their theory of the case and use evidence and testimony to support their positions.

The plaintiff will have to prove each necessary element of his or her cause of action, while the defendant will try to prove that one or more essential elements of the plaintiff's case is

( ) TALKING TO A LAWYER

Q. I attended a settlement conference, and the judge essentially told me that I had no chance of winning my case. I ended up settling, and now I regret it; I think I deserved the opportunity for a trial. Is there anything I can do about this now?

A. Once a case is settled, there is very little you can do—unless the case has not been dismissed and a judgment has not been granted for either side. If the judge has not accepted the settlement, you can try rejecting it in writing based on your feeling that it was not entered into freely and voluntarily. However, the other side will surely oppose your request and try to hold you to your agreement. This will be financially and emotionally costly. Therefore, you should reevaluate your feelings about the settlement. A compromise requires each side to give up something. Often, a known result is better than the risk of something worse. For this reason, lawyers often say that "a bad settlement is better than a good lawsuit."

—Answer by Judge Goldstein,
Law Offices of Alvin H. Goldstein Jr.,
San Rafael, California

missing. For example, in a case about a waiter spilling scalding coffee on the lap of a customer and causing severe burns, the plaintiff might seek to prove that:

1. The waiter had a legal duty to be careful not to spill the coffee.

2. The waiter failed to exercise the level of care that the law requires.

3. The spilled coffee was the cause of the burns that the customer suffered.

4. The restaurant is responsible for failing to properly train or supervise the waiter.

5. The damages sustained by the customer amount to $2,400 in emergency room bills, $185 in dry-cleaning bills,

$8,900 in lost wages, and $1,600 for pain and suffering. The customer might also seek $75,000 in punitive damages because the restaurant has spilled hot coffee on other customers and did not take steps to ensure that this would not happen again.

The plaintiff must prove his or her case by a **preponderance of the evidence**. This means that the judge or jury must be persuaded that the greater weight of the evidence favors the plaintiff. This does not depend on the number of witnesses or amount of physical evidence, but on whether the plaintiff's evidence is convincing.

In the above example, the defendants—the waiter and the restaurant—might try to prove that a necessary element of the plaintiff's case is missing, and might try to convince the judge or jury that the plaintiff has not proven his or her case.

Each side will bring evidence to support its case, which in the above example might include photographs, doctor's records, testimony from burn experts, and witness statements. The lawyers for each side may make arguments about how the law should apply to the facts.

▶ **A GUIDE TO GOOD BEHAVIOR**

When you are in court, no matter what side you are on, keep the following tips in mind:

- Be courteous to the judge and the opposing party (including lawyers) at all times

- Don't interrupt the other side

- Wait for the judge or your lawyer to recognize you before speaking

- Don't yell, curse, or roll your eyes

- Turn off your cell phone or pager in the courtroom

- Dress appropriately, in order to demonstrate that you respect yourself, your case, and the court. A suit is always appropriate attire.

Juries

Some civil cases are decided by a jury. Whether you are entitled to a jury trial will depend on the type of case and the law of the state where your case is pending. In the federal system, a party may request a jury trial if a case meets certain criteria. If neither party requests a trial by jury, the judge will hear the case. In civil jury trials, juries may consist of between six and twelve persons. Sometimes the size of a jury can be increased or decreased by agreement of both parties.

The trial jury is chosen from a list called a **venire** (also called a **jury pool**) that has been compiled by the court. During jury selection, the court clerk generally instructs people on the jury list to sit in the jury box. The judge usually makes a brief statement explaining the kind of case to be tried, and asks each potential juror whether there is any reason he or she cannot serve. The judge or lawyers then ask questions, designed to reveal whether the potential jurors have any knowledge of the case or life experiences that might cause them to be biased. This questioning of potential jurors is known as **voir dire**.

If the lawyer for either side learns that a juror may have preconceived ideas about how the case should be decided, he or she can ask the judge to dismiss that juror **for cause**. For example, a juror can be dismissed for cause if he or she is a close relative of one of the parties or one of the lawyers, or if he or she works for a company that is immediately affected by the lawsuit. Each lawyer may request the dismissal for cause of an unlimited number of jurors. The judge will consider each request and decide whether it should be allowed.

In addition to challenges for cause, each lawyer has a specific number of **peremptory challenges**. These challenges permit a lawyer to excuse a potential juror without stating a cause. However, peremptory challenges cannot be used to discriminate against potential jurors on the basis of race or sex. Each side is limited to a certain number of peremptory challenges.

When both parties have agreed upon the jury, the jurors are

(i) JURY DUTY

Even people who have never been involved in litigation may have first-hand experience with courts from participating in jury duty. The way in which people are selected for jury duty varies from state to state. In many states, a list is compiled from voter registration or driver's license lists. In these states, the people selected are sent a summons and ordered to report for jury service at the court.

If you are called to jury duty, it is important to respond to the summons. Thomas Jefferson called the jury system "the only anchor yet imagined by man by which a government can be held to the principles of its constitution." Serving on a jury gives you a chance to participate in our legal system.

---

sworn in by the court clerk. Those jurors who have not been selected are excused. Once impaneled, the jury's role is to listen to the lawyers and the witnesses carefully in order to decide the facts of the case. In some jurisdictions, jurors have the right to take notes and submit questions to witnesses via the judge.

Opening Statements

After the jury is sworn, the parties have an opportunity to make opening statements. **Opening statements** are like previews of the case to come. The plaintiff's side goes first. In the spilled-coffee example, the plaintiff's lawyer might deliver an opening statement as follows: "You will see evidence demonstrating that the defendant, Mr. Lopez, carelessly spilled scalding hot coffee into the lap of Mr. Engstrom, burning the skin of his thighs." The defendant's opening statement is a preview of the defense. In the same example, the defendant's opening statement might be as follows: "You will see evidence and hear testimony demonstrating that Mr. Lopez, through no fault of his own, spilled cof-

( ) TALKING TO A LAWYER

Q. I understand that juries decide questions of fact and judges decide questions of law. If I have the choice, am I better off with a jury or a judge? How can I evaluate this?

A. You really can't. Let your lawyer decide. If you don't have a lawyer and are representing yourself, you are better off letting a judge hear your case without a jury. This is known as a **bench trial**. If a judge is hearing your case without a jury, he or she might be more lenient regarding procedural irregularities and other technical requirements of a trial—including what evidence you can present (i.e., **admissibility**). With trials in front of a jury, most judges tend to be more strict. You won't be allowed simply to tell your story to a jury and let it decide your fate. Do you understand how a jury is selected? Do you know what voir dire is, and how it is conducted? Do you know what hearsay is? Do you know the other rules of evidence? Do you know how to present a trial memorandum or points for charge, or make an opening and closing statement? I didn't think so. So don't try to weather a jury trial on your own; consult a lawyer.

—Answer by Judge Robert Shenkin,
Court of Common Pleas of Chester County,
West Chester, Pennsylvania

fee onto himself and Mr. Engstrom. This occurred when Mr. Engstrom's cell phone vibrated, causing Mr. Engstrom to suddenly move and bump his elbow into Mr. Lopez, causing the coffee to spill." The opening statements set the tone of the trial, and give the jury its first impression of the case.

Evidence

The heart of the case is called the **case in chief**. This is the part of the case in which the parties present evidence to the judge or jury to support their versions of events.

The lawyer for the plaintiff begins the presentation of evidence by calling witnesses. The questions the lawyer asks of his or her own witnesses are referred to as **direct examination**. In direct examination, witnesses may testify to what they know or saw. For example, a lawyer might ask a witness, "What did you see on the afternoon of May 12?" Witnesses may also be called upon to identify documents, pictures, or other items introduced into evidence.

After the plaintiff has examined a witness, the defendant or his lawyer will have an opportunity to question that same witness. This process is called **cross-examination**. Cross-examination gives the defendant an opportunity to test the credibility of the witness's testimony, and to extract information from the plaintiff's witness that might hurt the plaintiff. During cross-examination, lawyers often try to demonstrate a witness's prejudice, bias, unreliability or dishonesty. For example, a lawyer might ask a witness whether he is friends with the plaintiff, or if the witness stands to benefit if the plaintiff wins the case. Or a lawyer might ask whether the witness has ever been convicted of a crime, in order to call into question that witness's believability (or **credibility**).

OBJECTION!

In a trial, strict rules govern the kind of evidence that may be admitted, and lawyers who appear in court are skilled at knowing what evidence is allowed. The other side may object to evidence (such as documents or the testimony of a witness) by stating a specific legal reason for the objection. Usually, the judge will **sustain** or **overrule** an objection immediately. If the objection is sustained, the lawyer must rephrase the question in a proper form or ask another question. If the objection is overruled and the witness answers the question, the lawyer who raised the objection may appeal the judge's ruling after the trial is over.

Presentation of Defense Evidence and Rebuttal

After the plaintiff's side has presented its case in chief, it is the defendant's turn to present his or her case. The defendant may call witnesses and introduce evidence to attack one or more necessary elements of the plaintiff's case. The plaintiff will be given an opportunity to cross-examine the defendant's witnesses. At the conclusion of the defendant's case, the plaintiff can present rebuttal witnesses or evidence to refute evidence presented by the defendant.

Closing Arguments

During closing arguments, the plaintiff and the defendant address the judge or jury one last time. The **closing arguments** are summaries that tie together testimony and evidence from different sources into a logical story. In the spilled-coffee example, the closing argument from the plaintiff's lawyer might include the following: "You heard Mr. Engstrom describe how he was injured when the defendant spilled hot coffee in his lap. Nick Collins saw what happened and confirmed Mr. Engstrom's explanation of how the incident happened. Then we heard from Dr. Shrey, who testified about the severity of the burns that resulted from the hot coffee." Closing statements are the parties' last chance to convince the judge or jury that their version of events is correct.

Instructions to the Jury

In a jury trial, the judge will give the jury instructions in order to guide its deliberations. The judge will read these instructions to the jury, which is commonly referred to as the judge's **charge** to the jury. In giving the instructions, the judge may state the issues presented by the case, and define any terms that may be unfamiliar to the jurors. In state courts, judges are not allowed to comment on the facts or evidence in a case. The judge will advise the jury that the jury is the sole judge of the facts and the credibility of witnesses. He or she will instruct the jurors to base their conclusions on the evidence presented during the trial. The judge will also point out that the instructions contain the judge's interpretation of the law, and that jurors must abide by the law as determined by the judge.

For example, the jury instructions in a civil case arising out of a sports brawl might read as follows:

1. First, you must determine whether Matthew punched Juan on the morning of the football game.

2. If you decide that Matthew punched Juan, you must decide if Matthew was adequately provoked.

3. State law defines "adequate provocation" as "the response of a person in the heat of the moment, which a reasonable person would have to a similar stimulus without prior agitation or use of alcohol."

4. If you find that Matthew was not adequately provoked and that he punched Juan, you must calculate the damages for which Matthew is liable as a result of punching Juan. The state grants damages to victims of unprovoked violence for medical bills, lost wages, and pain and suffering.

Jury Deliberations

After receiving instructions, the jury will retire to the jury room to make a decision. In most courts, the jury will elect one of the jurors as the **presiding juror**. This person's role is to preside over discussions and votes by the jurors. In many states, the jury in a civil case does not have to reach a unanimous decision.

Verdict

After the jury has reached a decision, all of the participants in the case reconvene in the courtroom. In many courts, the judge will review the decision of the jury before it is announced. The presiding juror, the judge, or the court clerk will then announce the verdict in the case. If the jury finds for the plaintiff, the jury will also determine the dollar amount of damages the defendant owes the plaintiff.

Judgment

The decision of the jury does not take effect until the judge enters a **judgment** on the decision that can be filed in public records. The judge may have the authority to increase or decrease the amount of damages ordered by the jury, or to make other modifications before entering judgment.

APPEALS

A popular misconception is that cases are always appealed. But in most states, a losing party does not have an automatic right of appeal. Rather, there must be a legal basis for the appeal, and the losing party must be able to point to an important error in the trial that influenced the decision.

If an appellate court agrees to hear an appeal, it usually will not review the factual findings of the court. It assumes that a judge or jury is in the best position to decide questions of fact. As a result, it will not recall witnesses or consider new evidence. Appeals usually are based on arguments regarding errors in procedure or errors in the judge's interpretation of the law.

ENFORCEMENT

Once you receive a judgment in your favor, the first thing to do is hope that the **judgment debtor** (the person who lost the case) cooperates with the ruling and gives you what the court says you deserve. Unfortunately, obtaining a judgment in your favor can be considerably easier than collecting the money you are owed under the judgment. If the defendant does not cooperate, collecting on judgments can be a very time-consuming and difficult job.

If a judgment has been granted in your favor and the judgment debtor doesn't pay, you will probably need to work with an **enforcement officer**—who may be a marshal or sheriff—or your lawyer to help you collect your judgment. It is important to follow the rules of enforcement collection within your jurisdiction. It is never a good idea to try to collect a judgment yourself from an angry and uncooperative debtor.

Jurisdictions also have their own rules about how enforcement officers are paid. Sometimes enforcement officers collect a set fee from the creditor. Sometimes they collect a percentage of the recovered property, and sometimes their fee is paid by the state or court.

Wage Garnishment

One way that a lawyer or enforcement officer can collect your judgment is by **income execution**, also known as **wage garnishment**. If the judgment debtor receives a regular income, the lawyer or enforcement officer can obtain a court order requiring the debtor's employer to garnish his or her paycheck. Once the employer has received notice to withhold part of the judgment debtor's wages, the employer is under a legal obligation to comply. Checks will be sent to the court, which then will be passed on to you. This means that you will receive part of the judgment debtor's income every payday, until the judgment debt is paid. The amount or percentage that can be garnished from a judgment debtor's wages is set by law and differs from state to state.

▶ **SHOW ME THE MONEY**

If you cannot locate a debtor's assets or wage source, there are services available to track property or state records and find property owned by the debtor. Your lawyer should be able to help you trace the judgment debtor's assets.

Seizure of Personal Property

Enforcement officers can also seize personal property and cash from a judgment creditor's possession. In these instances, the marshal or sheriff actually goes to the creditor's property and collects personal property, which is sold so that the proceeds of sale can satisfy your judgment.

The enforcement officer might charge you for the storage and shipment of the personal property. For example, a sheriff who seizes a Corvette might charge you for the tow truck, storage, and subsequent costs of auctioning the vehicle.

Liens

Most jurisdictions do not allow enforcement officers to seize the **real property** (real estate) of a judgment debtor. However, you can ask the court to issue an order for a judgment lien. A **lien** is a legal claim against the debtor's property, which appears on the certificate of title to the land. The lien limits the debtor's ability to sell the property or obtain a mortgage. A lien also gives you the right to sell the property to satisfy the debt if it is not otherwise paid.

⚠️ YOU CAN'T GET BLOOD FROM A TURNIP

The unfortunate reality is that some people or businesses are judgment-proof, because they don't have any money, property, or income. Even if you win in court, you cannot enforce your judgment against a judgment-proof debtor, because he or she cannot pay, regardless of who attempts to collect. When you are deciding whether and whom to sue, think carefully about whether the defendant has the resources to pay a judgment.

THE WORLD AT YOUR FINGERTIPS

• You can find a great general guide to the courts on the U.S. Courts website, at *www.uscourts.gov/library.html*. It includes information on commonly used terms, court fees, legal forms, and policies, in addition to court-related publications and reports. The site also provides links to the websites of other courts at *www.uscourts.gov/courtlinks*.

• The ABA Division for Public Education has published a short guide to how courts work. You can download the guide at *www.abanet.org/publiced/practical/home.html*.

REMEMBER THIS

• Civil cases include personal-injury cases, contract disputes, and disputes over property. In most civil cases, the plaintiff is seeking money damages.

• Statutes of limitations establish time frames within which plaintiffs must file their cases. If you wish to file a lawsuit, act quickly to ensure that you file in a timely fashion.

• If you anticipate litigation, save evidence. Take pictures, save e-mails, and write down the names and contact information of witnesses.

• This chapter contains general information about pretrial and trial procedures. However, specific rules will vary from court to court. Your lawyer can provide you with more detailed information about how things work in your particular jurisdiction.

• Enforcing a judgment can be difficult. An enforcement officer can help you collect the money you are owed under a judgment.

CHAPTER 7

Finding and Working With a Lawyer

How to Find the Right Lawyer for Your Case

Amit is involved in a dispute with his landlord. A tree on the rental property fell on Amit's truck during a storm, and caused $7,000 worth of damage. Amit tried to negotiate with the landlord about payment for repairs. The landlord delayed meeting Amit for weeks, and then said that the damage was not his responsibility.

Amit decides to talk to a lawyer about whether he has a legal right to payment, and what he can do to pursue it. Amit has never hired a lawyer before. How can he find a lawyer who might be able to help him? What questions should he ask his lawyer? How much will it cost to hire a lawyer to assist him in resolving his dispute?

The need for legal services can be said to exist along a vast continuum. At one end of the spectrum are disputes you can handle on your own, without the assistance of a lawyer. At the other end—if circumstances and laws are complex, if you're injured, or if you are at risk of losing valuable rights—you require a lawyer's guidance and representation. Where does your legal matter fall on this continuum? When do you need a lawyer? How can you find one? How do you work with one? This chapter, which is drawn from the *ABA Family Legal Guide* (see the end of this chapter for more information), can help you make the best choices when working with a lawyer.

WHEN DO YOU NEED A LAWYER?

When faced with a legal problem, the first question many people ask is: "Do I need to hire a lawyer?" As you can probably guess, the answer is: "It depends." The need for a lawyer varies with the circumstances of each situation. In making a decision, you may want to consider the following questions:

• **How important is the issue?** For example, in a divorce, if there is a lot of money in dispute or if custody of children is at stake, a lawyer's help is very important. Conversely, if the dollar amount in dispute is low and no other important matters are at issue, a lawyer's help may not be necessary. If your case lies somewhere between these two extremes, you need to compare the benefits that a lawyer could provide with the costs you would incur for legal services.

• **How well do you understand the issue?** If you have been served with legal papers, and you don't know what the papers mean or what to do next, consult a lawyer. However, if you understand the legal issues and the steps you need to take, you may not need a lawyer.

• **How emotionally involved are you?** An old adage states, "A person who represents himself has a fool for a client." Much of the time—indeed, maybe most of the time—this adage is correct. But some people are good at representing themselves. A key issue in deciding whether to represent yourself is your level of emotional involvement and your ability to assume a detached view of the controversy. If you are very angry at the other party, it may be best to have independent legal help to present the case in an organized, professional way. On the other hand, if you can keep a lid on your emotions and present logical arguments in negotiations or in court, then you may be able to represent yourself effectively.

• **How user-friendly is the court system?** Some courts, such as small-claims courts, are designed to help people handle their own legal disputes. Such courts may provide forms with clear explanations to help people initiate or respond to legal actions. Court personnel might also be able to provide you with direct assistance, guiding you step-by-step and providing information about your legal rights. In other court systems, procedures may be complex and difficult to follow—even for lawyers. To gauge the extent to which a particular court system accommodates

◯ TALKING TO A LAWYER

Q. When is it in my interest not to hire a lawyer? Is it ever best for me to represent myself in a trial?

A. Only if you are the plaintiff, the amount involved is relatively small, and you are not being sued on a counterclaim (which would mean that you are also a defendant). Otherwise, get a lawyer. If you don't know one, call your local bar association and ask if it operates or knows of a local lawyer referral service. Picking a lawyer is very difficult. You should always meet with at least two—and preferably three—lawyers before hiring one. Explain your situation to each of the lawyers, and see what response you get. Ask about fees. Never hire a lawyer who won't discuss fees with you before you hire him or her. After you hire a lawyer, get a written **engagement letter**. This letter should spell out the purpose for which you are hiring the lawyer, and the fees and other costs and expenses that will be your responsibility.

—Answer by Judge Robert Shenkin,
Court of Common Pleas of Chester County,
West Chester, Pennsylvania

people who represent themselves, visit the courthouse or call the clerk of court with some polite questions.

• **How much does legal representation cost?** Of course, an important factor in deciding whether to hire a lawyer is the cost of legal representation. When involved in any legal dispute, you will need to perform a cost-benefit analysis and ask: "Is pursuit of this case—or some issue in the case—sufficiently important to be worth the cost of hiring a lawyer?" If the stakes are high, full-scale representation may be worth the money, and may even save dollars—or something else—of great value. If the stakes are small, however, legal representation may not be cost-effective.

If you consider these questions and are still in doubt about

▶ GET HELP EARLY

Don't ignore invoices or letters threatening legal action; legal problems won't just go away. When dealing with legal issues, an ounce of prevention is worth many dollars and anxious hours of cure. Waiting to contact a lawyer until a legal problem has escalated to crisis proportions can lead to unnecessary anxiety, and may make the problem more difficult and expensive to solve. Lawyers should be thought of as preventers of legal problems, not just solvers.

whether to hire a lawyer, err on the side of caution and at least make an appointment to talk with a lawyer.

If you avoid calling a lawyer because you are trying to avoid litigation, you may be hurting yourself. Your lawyer might be able to save you from litigation by working with you in a negotiation, mediation, or arbitration. If you call a lawyer as a last resort, it may already be too late. A lawyer may not be able to protect you after you have lost your rights.

FINDING A LAWYER

You've thought about it carefully, you've spoken to friends, and you've decided that you need to contact a lawyer to discuss a legal issue. The next question is—how to find one? This section will give you some tips on what to look for when choosing a lawyer. If you do your homework, you can hire the lawyer who has the experience and expertise to help you with your problem. Nothing you hear or read can tell you which particular lawyer will be best for you. Instead, you must judge for yourself. Don't be afraid to trust your gut instinct.

Your lawyer will be helping to solve your problems, so the first requirement is that you must feel comfortable enough to tell him or her, honestly and completely, all the facts of your case. You will also need to take into account:

• The lawyer's experience and area of expertise. Ask about your lawyer's areas of concentration, and about the types of cases he or she generally handles.

• The lawyer's office location, and whether meeting with the lawyer will be convenient for you

• The lawyer's prices and fee structures

• Whether the lawyer is willing to provide the legal services that fit your needs and budget

Where to Start

There are many ways to find a reliable lawyer. One of the best ways is to obtain a recommendation from a trusted friend, relative, or business associate. Be aware, however, that each legal case is different, and that a lawyer who is right for someone else may not necessarily be right for you or your legal problem.

Most communities have referral services to help people find lawyers; see the section titled "The World at Your Fingertips" at the end of this chapter for more details. A referral service usually can recommend a lawyer in the area to evaluate your situation. Several services offer help to groups with unique legal needs, such as the elderly, immigrants, victims of domestic violence, or persons with disabilities. In addition, bar associations in most communities make referrals according to specific areas of law, and can help you find a lawyer with the right experience and practice concentration. Many referral services also have competency requirements for lawyers who wish to have referrals in particular areas of law.

Still, these services are not a surefire way to find the right lawyer. The reason is that some services make referrals without reference to a lawyer's specialty or level of experience. For this reason, you may want to seek out a lawyer referral service that participates in the ABA-sponsored certification program. This program uses a logo to identify lawyer referral programs that comply with certain quality standards developed by the ABA.

If you are looking for low-cost legal help, several legal assistance programs offer inexpensive or free legal services to the poor. Look in the Yellow Pages under "Legal Aid," or search online (see the list of resources at the end of this chapter). Most legal-aid programs have special guidelines for eligibility, often based on where you live, the size of your family, and your income. Some legal-aid offices have their own staff lawyers, and others operate with volunteer lawyers. Note that people do not have an automatic right to a free lawyer in civil legal matters, and legal aid lacks the resources to meet all the legal needs of the poor. If you cannot afford a lawyer, read the "Types of Fees" section of this chapter for information about contingency fee arrangements. You may want to hire a lawyer who only gets paid if you obtain a settlement or judgment.

Lastly, departments and agencies of the state and federal governments often have staff lawyers who help the general public for free in limited situations. Your local United States Attorney's Office might be able to provide guidance about federal

LOOK FOR UNBUNDLED LEGAL SERVICES

Increasingly, lawyers offer clients what is known as a **limited scope of representation** or **unbundled legal services**. In these types of arrangements, a lawyer "partners" with a client to provide certain services. For example, a lawyer might act as a legal coach for a client who plans to do the legal work on his own and represent himself in court. Or the lawyer may contract with the client for the sole purpose of negotiating a resolution or filling out the papers and documents relating to a legal matter. When people hire lawyers on an unbundled basis, it reduces costs and allows clients more decision-making power. Finding a lawyer who will unbundle services can be a good strategy for people who don't need comprehensive representation, but who are not comfortable doing everything themselves. Your lawyer can discuss these issues with you, and help you decide the best alternative for your case.

(i) TRANSACTIONAL LAWYERS AND LITIGATION LAWYERS

There are two main types of civil lawyers: transactional lawyers and litigation lawyers. **Transactional lawyers** are essentially contract writers and dealmakers. They often work in situations where the goal is to write good contracts and make favorable deals to prevent lawsuits. For example, if you are opening a small business, a transactional lawyer can advise you on the pros and cons of including a mandatory arbitration clause in your commercial lease. A transactional lawyer might also help you set up a trust fund, assist you in buying real estate, or give you advice about the tax implications of selling goods over the Internet.

Transactional lawyers are like preventive medicine; they help you avoid disputes. The transactional lawyer is not battling with other parties; rather, he or she works to minimize the chance that a legal dispute will arise, while ensuring that you will be in the best possible legal position in the event of a dispute.

If you do become involved in a dispute—for example, if you breach a contract, if you want to make a complaint about discrimination at work, or if you want to challenge a relative's will—then you will probably want to work with a **litigation lawyer**. A litigation lawyer is trained to serve as your advocate in the dispute, whether you are involved in mediation, arbitration, or a court case.

laws. It might also guide you to federal agencies that deal with specific concerns, such as environmental protection problems or discrimination in employment or housing. The state attorney general also may provide free guidance to the public regarding state laws. For example, some state attorney general's offices maintain consumer protection departments. Similarly, counties, cities, and townships often employ government lawyers who can provide the public with guidance about local laws. Some of these local offices also offer consumer protection assistance. To find such agencies, check the government listings in your phone book, or search online.

Meeting with Your Prospective Lawyer

During an initial consultation, a lawyer usually will meet with you briefly or talk with you by phone so the two of you can get acquainted. This meeting is a chance to assess your prospective lawyer before making a final hiring decision. In many cases, there is no fee charged for an initial consultation. However, to be on the safe side, ask about fees before setting up your first appointment.

During this preliminary meeting, think about whether you want to hire the lawyer. Many people feel nervous or intimidated when meeting lawyers, but remember that you're the one doing the hiring, and what's most important is that you're satisfied with what you're getting for your money. Before you make any hiring decisions, you might want to ask certain questions to aid in your evaluation. Some possible questions are suggested below.

Ask about the lawyer's experience and areas of practice. How long has the lawyer and the firm been practicing law? What kinds of legal problems does the lawyer handle most often? Are most clients individuals or businesses? Ask your prospective lawyer who else, if anyone, will be working on your case. Ask if staff such as paralegals or law clerks will be used in researching or preparing the case. If so, will there be separate charges for their services? Who will be consulted if the lawyer is unsure about some aspects of your case? Will the lawyer recommend another lawyer or firm if this one is unable to handle your case?

Occasionally a lawyer will suggest that someone else in the same firm or an outside lawyer handle your specific problem. Perhaps the original lawyer is too busy to give your case the full attention it deserves, or maybe your problem requires another person's expertise. No one likes to feel that he or she is being passed around from one lawyer to another. However, most reassignments within firms occur for a good reason. Do not hesitate to request a meeting with the new lawyer to make sure you are comfortable with him or her.

When people hire lawyers, one of their most common complaints is the high cost of legal services. However, while good legal counsel will cost you money, you can eliminate some of the frustration and surprise of high costs by having clear conversations about fees early in the process. Make sure you ask your prospective lawyer about how fees are charged—by the hour, by the case, or by the amount won. How much will it cost if the lawyer handles the case from start to finish? When must you pay the bill? Can you pay it in installments? Ask for a written statement explaining how and what fees will be charged, and a monthly statement detailing specific services rendered and the charge for each service if your case is prolonged.

If you are hiring a lawyer to help you resolve a dispute, it is important that you ask for the lawyer's opinion of your case's strengths and weaknesses. Will the lawyer most likely settle your case, or is it likely that the case will go to trial? What are the advantages and disadvantages of settlement? Of mediation? Of going to trial? What kind of experience does the lawyer have in trial work? If you lose at trial, will the lawyer be willing to appeal the decision? Beware of any lawyer who guarantees a big settlement or assures a victory in court. Remember that there are at least two sides to every legal issue, and many factors can affect the resolution of a dispute.

Remember: When you hire a lawyer, you are paying for legal *advice*. Your lawyer should make no major decision about whether and how to go on with the case without your permission. Pay special attention to whether the lawyer seems willing and able to explain the case to you, and whether he or she answers your questions clearly and completely. Ask him or her what information will be supplied to you. How, and how often, will the lawyer keep you informed about the progress of your case? Will the lawyer send you copies of any documents pertaining to your case? Can you help keep fees down by partnering with your lawyer and performing some of the tasks yourself?

⚠ ADVERTISING

Newspapers, telephone directories, radio, television ads, and direct mail can all provide you with the names of lawyers who may be appropriate for your legal needs. Some ads will help you determine a lawyer's area of expertise. Other ads will quote a fee or price range for handling a specific type of "simple" case. However, don't take everything you read at face value, and keep in mind that your case may not have a simple solution. If a lawyer quotes a fee, be certain you know exactly what services and expenses the charge does and does not include.

Your first meeting is the best time to ask about resolving potential problems that may arise between you and your lawyer. Find out if the lawyer will agree to arbitration or mediation if a serious dispute arises between the two of you. In some states, it is mandatory for lawyers to agree to arbitrate or mediate certain types of disputes with their clients. Most state bar associations have arbitration or mediation committees that will help resolve disputes over fees between you and your lawyer.

Before hiring a lawyer, consider interviewing several candidates. While it may seem tedious, your decision will be more informed if you consider several lawyers before you make a decision. Even if you think you will be satisfied with the first lawyer you interview, you will ultimately feel better about your choice if you consider more than one option.

UNDERSTANDING LEGAL FEES AND COSTS

Legal services can be expensive. We all know that. But there are steps you can take to avoid surprises when the bill arrives. Talk to your lawyer about fees and expenses, and make sure you un-

▶ **TALK ABOUT FEES**

Although money is often a touchy subject in our society, fees and other charges should be discussed with your lawyer early in the case. You can avoid future problems by having a clear understanding of the fees to be charged, and by documenting that understanding in writing before any legal work has started. If fees are to be charged on an hourly basis, ask for a complete itemized list and an explanation of charges each time the lawyer bills you. It is important to avoid a situation in which you pay a retainer but are unable to pay all of your legal bills. This will either lead to the lawyer withdrawing from your case and leaving you to represent yourself, or the lawyer working without getting paid. Neither situation is likely to meet your needs.

The high cost of legal services may surprise some clients—especially in the case of a simple job, such as preparing a one-page legal document or providing basic advice. But remember that when you hire a lawyer, you are paying for his or her expertise as well as time.

derstand all the information he or she provides. It's best to ask for this type of information in writing before legal work starts. But remember: Fees cannot always be estimated exactly, because unforeseen events may arise during the course of your case.

In the most common type of billing arrangement, lawyers charge a set amount for each hour or fraction of an hour they spend working on your case. Whether this set amount is reasonable depends on several things. Experienced lawyers tend to charge more per hour than those with less experience—but they also may take less time to perform the same legal work. In addition, the same lawyer will usually charge more for time spent in the courtroom than for hours spent in the office or library.

The fee charged by a lawyer should be reasonable from an objective point of view. The fee should be tied to specific services rendered, time invested, the level of expertise provided, and the difficulty of the matter. In addition, the reasonableness of a fee will depend upon

- the time and work required by the lawyer and any assistants;
- the complexity of the legal issues presented;
- how much other lawyers in the area charge for similar work;
- the total value of the claim or settlement and the results of the case;
- the lawyer's experience, reputation, and ability; and
- the amount of other work the lawyer had to turn down to take on a particular case.

Costs are expenses incurred in addition to your lawyer's fees. These include the court clerk's costs for filing complaints or petitions, the sheriff's costs for serving legal summonses, and the costs of mailing and copying documents, telephone calls, and expert witnesses such as doctors. These expenses may not be included in your legal fee, and you may have to pay them regardless of your fee arrangement. Usually your lawyer will pay these costs as needed, billing you at regular intervals or at the close of your case.

Types of Fees

A **contingency fee** is a fee that you pay only if your case is successful. Lawyers and clients use contingency fee arrangements in cases involving money damages—most often in cases involving personal injury or workers' compensation. Many states strictly forbid this billing method in criminal cases and in most cases involving family law matters.

In a contingency fee arrangement, a lawyer agrees to accept a fixed percentage (often one third) of the amount recovered. If you win the case, the lawyer's fee comes out of the money awarded to you. If you lose, neither you nor the lawyer will get any money, but you will not be required to pay your lawyer for the work done on the case.

On the other hand, win or lose, you probably will have to pay court filing charges, the costs related to deposing witnesses, and similar expenses. By entering into a contingency fee agreement, both you and your lawyer expect to collect some unknown amount of money. However, because many personal-injury actions involve considerable and often complicated legal work, this may be less expensive than paying an hourly rate. You should clearly understand your options before entering into a contingency fee arrangement.

Not all contingency fee arrangements are the same. An important consideration is whether the lawyer deducts costs and expenses from the amount won before or after you pay the contingency fee. For example, suppose Brian hires Arwen Attorney to represent him, agreeing that Arwen will receive one third of the final amount—in this case, $12,000. Miscellaneous expenses associated with Brian's case total $2,100. If Brian pays Arwen her contingency fee *before* expenses are deducted from the award, the fee will be calculated as follows:

$12,000	Total amount recovered in the case
− 4,000	Contingency fee (one third) for Arwen Attorney
$8,000	
−2,100	Payment for expenses and costs
$5,900	Amount that Brian recovers

However, if Brian pays Arwen her contingency fee *after* other legal expenses and costs are deducted from the award, the amount of Brian's recovery will be quite different:

$12,000	Total amount recovered in the case
−2,100	Payment for expenses and costs
$9,900	
−3,300	Contingency fee (one third) for Arwen Attorney
$6,600	Amount that Brian recovers

These calculations demonstrate that Brian will collect an additional $700 if the agreement provides for Arwen Attorney to collect her share *after* Brian pays for miscellaneous legal expenses.

Many lawyers prefer to be paid before they subtract the cost of expenses from an award, but this point is often negotiable. Of course, these matters should be settled before you hire a lawyer. If you agree to pay a contingency fee, your lawyer usually is required to provide a written explanation of the agreement, clearly stating how he or she will deduct costs. If you and your lawyer agree to a contingency fee arrangement, the method of settling your case may affect the amount of your lawyer's fee. If the lawyer settles the case before going to trial, less legal work may be required. On the other hand, the lawyer may have to prepare for trial, with all its costs and expenses, before a settlement can be negotiated. You can try to negotiate an agreement in which the lawyer accepts a lower percentage if he or she settles the case before a lawsuit is filed in court. However, many lawyers might not agree to these types of terms.

A **fixed fee** is a set amount charged for routine legal work. In some situations, this amount may be set by law or by the judge handling a case. Since advertising by lawyers is becoming more popular, you are likely to see ads offering fixed-fee services—for

▶ **SOME TIPS ON MINIMIZING FEES**

- Be organized. Make sure you bring all relevant documents to any meeting with your lawyer, so that your lawyer's time isn't wasted.

- Be brief. If your lawyer is charging you by the hour, don't waste time with irrelevant conversation or long-winded explanations.

- If your lawyer is working on something for you, don't call every time you have a minor question. Instead, save up a few questions to ask all at once.

- Ask your lawyer if there is anything you can do to help. For example, can you write some letters, make some phone calls, or change the title of some assets?

- Ask your lawyer to alert you if the cost of your case starts to escalate beyond the cost discussed.

- Ask for an itemized bill so you can see the cost of each service provided.

example, "Simple Divorce: $350" or "Bankruptcy: from $550." However, do not assume that fixed fees will constitute the entire amount of your final bill. Advertised prices often do not include court costs and other expenses.

Retainers

If you pay a small amount of money regularly to ensure that a lawyer is available for any legal service you might require, then you are said to have a lawyer **on retainer**. Businesses and people who routinely have a lot of legal work use retainers. By paying a retainer, a client receives routine consultations and general legal advice whenever needed. If a legal matter requires courtroom time or many hours of work, the client may need to pay more than the retainer amount. Retainer agreements should always be in writing. Most people do not see a lawyer regularly, and do not need to have a lawyer on retainer.

Note that having a lawyer on retainer is not the same thing as paying a **retainer fee.** Sometimes a lawyer will ask a client to pay a fee in advance before he or she will perform any legal work. This payment is referred to as a retainer fee, and is in effect a down payment that will be applied toward the total fee billed.

HOW TO REDUCE LEGAL COSTS

There are several steps you can take to reduce the amount of fees and costs you must pay to a lawyer. First, answer all of your lawyer's questions fully and honestly. Remember that the attorney-client privilege binds your lawyer to maintain in the strictest confidence almost anything you reveal during your private discussions. You should tell your lawyer the complete details of your case, even those that embarrass you. Not only will you feel better, but you will also save on legal fees in the long term, because your lawyer will be able to save time and do a better job. It is particularly important to reveal to your lawyer any facts that reflect poorly on you. These will almost certainly come out if your case progresses to mediation, arbitration, or trial.

Sometimes you may be able to reduce legal costs by helping with your own case. Many lawyers are receptive to unbundling legal services—that is, sharing the workload with clients. For example, maybe you can write the letter laying out your side of the case, and the lawyer need only review it, thus spending less time on your case and costing you less money. Often lawyers will provide advice, but will become heavily involved in a matter only if it goes to court. Let your lawyer know if you are willing to help out, such as by picking up or delivering documents or by making a few telephone calls.

You should not interfere with your lawyer's work. However, you might be able to speed up your case, reduce your legal costs, and keep yourself better informed by doing some of the work yourself. (For more information, see the Sidebar titled "Look for Unbundled Legal Services" earlier in this chapter.) Talk to your lawyer about whether such an arrangement might be appropriate in your case.

THE ETHICAL OBLIGATIONS OF LAWYERS

A lawyer's professional conduct is governed by the rules of professional conduct in the state or states where he or she is licensed to practice. These rules are usually administered by the state's highest court through its disciplinary board. The rules describe how lawyers should strive to improve the legal profession and uphold the law. They also give detailed rules of conduct for specific situations. If a lawyer's conduct falls below the standards set out in the rules, he or she can be disciplined by being **censured** or **reprimanded** (publicly or privately criticized); **suspended** (having his or her license to practice law revoked for a certain amount of time); or **disbarred** (having his or her license to practice law taken away indefinitely).

The law sets out punishments for anyone who breaks civil

▶ **SOME TIPS ON TALKING TO YOUR LAWYER**

- Before your first meeting with your lawyer, think about your legal problem, how you would like it resolved, and the outcome you hope to achieve.

- If your case involves other people, write down their names, addresses, and telephone numbers. Also jot down any specific facts or dates you think might be important, and any questions you want answered. By being organized, you will save time and money.

- Bring all relevant information and documents with you to any meeting with your lawyer, including contracts, leases, or any documents with which you have been served.

- If there has been a development in your case, don't wait until your next scheduled meeting to tell your lawyer about it. Tell your lawyer immediately of any changes that might be important. It might mean that the lawyer will have to take a totally different action—or no action at all—in your case.

- Let your lawyer know if you are unhappy with his or her work, and why.

- Don't wait for your lawyer to ask you about something; volunteer information that you think may be useful.

and criminal laws, and that includes lawyers. But because of the special position of trust and confidence involved in a lawyer-client relationship, lawyers may also be punished for things that are unethical, if not unlawful—such as revealing confidential information about a client, or representing clients whose interests are in conflict. Among the highest responsibilities a lawyer has is his or her obligation to a client. A number of strict rules and common sense guidelines define these responsibilities.

Competence

Every lawyer must aim to provide sound work. This requires the lawyer to analyze legal issues, research and study changing laws and legal trends, and otherwise represent the client effectively and professionally.

Following the Client's Instructions

A lawyer should advise a client of possible actions to be taken in a case, and then act according to the client's choice—even if the lawyer might have picked a different course of action. One of the few exceptions to this rule arises when a client asks for a lawyer's help in doing something illegal, such as lying in court or in a legal document. In these cases, the lawyer must inform the client of the legal effect of any planned wrongdoing and refuse to assist with it.

Diligence

Every lawyer must act carefully and in a timely manner in handling a client's legal problem. Unnecessary delays can often damage a case. If, because of overwork or for any other reason, a lawyer is unable to spend the required time and energy on a case, the lawyer should refuse to take the case. But note that legal matters can take a long time. If you have an extended case, chances are that delays will occur not because of your lawyer, but because of court scheduling or other factors outside of your lawyer's control.

Communication

A lawyer must be able to communicate effectively with a client. When a client asks for an explanation, the lawyer must provide it within a reasonable time. A lawyer must also inform a client about delays or other issues with a case as they arise.

▶ A CLIENT'S RESPONSIBILITIES

As in any successful relationship, a good lawyer-client relationship involves cooperation on both sides. As a client, you should do all you can to make sure you get the best possible legal help. This includes:

- **Being honest.** Be honest with your lawyer, and tell him or her all the facts of your case. Remind yourself of important points or questions by writing them down before talking with your lawyer.

- **Notifying the lawyer of changes.** Tell the lawyer promptly about any changes or new information you learn that may affect your case. And let your lawyer know if you change your address or telephone number.

- **Asking for clarification.** If you have any questions or are confused about something in your case, ask your lawyer for an explanation. This may go a long way toward putting your mind at ease—and will also help your lawyer to do a better job of handling your case.

- **Being realistic.** A lawyer can only handle your legal affairs. You may need the help of another professional—a banker, family counselor, accountant, or psychologist, for example—for problems that have no "legal" solution. After you have hired a lawyer you trust, be mindful of that trust, and remember that a lawyer's judgments are based on experience and training. Also, keep in mind that most legal matters cannot be resolved overnight. Give the system time to work.

- **Paying.** A client has the duty to pay promptly a fair and reasonable price for legal services. In fact, when a client fails to pay, in some situations his or her lawyer may have the right to stop working on the case. Even then, the lawyer must do whatever is reasonably possible to prevent the client's case from being harmed.

Fees

The amount a lawyer charges for legal work must be reasonable, and the client should be provided with details about all charges.

Confidentiality

With few exceptions, a lawyer may not tell anyone else what a client reveals about a case. Strict enforcement of this rule enables a client to discuss the details of his or her case openly and honestly with a lawyer, even if those details reveal embarrassing, damaging, or commercially sensitive information. **Attorney-client privilege** protects confidential information from being disclosed. Chapter 6 describes this rule in greater detail; your lawyer can also explain it to you.

Conflicts of Interest

A lawyer must be loyal to his or her client. This means that a lawyer cannot represent two clients who are on opposite sides of the same or related lawsuits. In addition, a lawyer ordinarily cannot represent a client whose interests would conflict with the lawyer's interests. For example, a lawyer may not be involved in writing a will for a client who leaves the lawyer substantial money or property in that will.

Keeping Clients' Property

If a lawyer is holding a client's money or property, it must be kept safely and separately from the lawyer's own funds and belongings. When a client asks for that property, the lawyer must return it immediately and in good condition. The lawyer must also keep careful records of money received for a client and, if asked, report such amounts promptly and accurately.

FILING A COMPLAINT AGAINST YOUR LAWYER

When you agree to hire a lawyer and that lawyer agrees to be your legal representative, a two-way relationship begins in which you both have the same goal: to satisfactorily resolve a legal matter. To this end, each of you must act responsibly toward the other. In a lawyer-client relationship, acting responsibly involves duties on both sides—and often involves some hard work.

You have a right to expect competent representation from your lawyer. However, every lawsuit has at least two sides. You cannot always blame your lawyer if your case does not turn out the way you thought it would. If you are unhappy with your lawyer, take a long cool look at the reasons for your unhappiness. Are you simply unhappy with the outcome, or are you unhappy with the way in which your lawyer handled the case? If your lawyer appears to have acted improperly, or failed to do something that you think he or she should have done, talk with him or her about it. You may be satisfied once you better understand the circumstances.

If you have tried talking with your lawyer, and your lawyer is unwilling to address your complaints, consider taking your legal affairs to another lawyer. You can decide whom to hire (and fire) as your lawyer. However, remember that when you fire a lawyer, you may be charged a reasonable amount for work he or she has already completed. Most documents held by your lawyer that relate to the case are yours, and you should ask for them if you want another lawyer to take over the matter. In some states, however, a lawyer may have some rights to hold on to a file until the client pays a reasonable amount for work completed on the case.

If you believe you have a valid complaint about how your lawyer has handled your case, consider informing the organization that governs licenses to practice law in your state. Usually this is the disciplinary board of the highest court in your state. In some states, the state bar association handles lawyer discipline. The board or the bar will either investigate the complaint or refer you to someone who can help. If your complaint concerns the amount your lawyer charged, you may be referred to a state or local bar association's fee arbitration service.

Filing a disciplinary complaint accusing your lawyer of un-ethical conduct is a serious matter. Be aware that making a complaint of this sort may punish the lawyer for misconduct, but it probably will not help you recover any money. If you have a case pending that your lawyer has mishandled, be sure to protect your rights by taking steps to see that your case is properly handled in the future.

If you believe that your lawyer has been negligent in handling your case—and that his or her negligence has cost you money, injured you, or violated your legal rights—you may be able to bring a **malpractice** suit against your lawyer.

If you believe that your lawyer has taken or improperly kept money or property that belongs to you, contact the state **client security fund**, **client indemnity fund** or **client assistance fund**. Your state or local bar association or state disciplinary board can tell you how to contact the fund that serves you. These funds may reimburse clients if a court finds that their lawyer has defrauded them. Lawyers pay fees to maintain such funds. Be aware, however, that most states' programs divide up the available money among all the clients who have proved cases against their lawyers. There is rarely enough money in the fund to pay 100 percent of every claim that is made.

THE WORLD AT YOUR FINGERTIPS

• The *American Bar Association Family Legal Guide* (3rd edition, 2004) contains more detailed information about working with a lawyer, and chapters on many different areas of the law. You can order the book from the ABA Web store, at *www.abanet. org/abastore*.

• To find a local lawyer referral program, call your bar association, look in the Yellow Pages, or visit *www.abanet.org/ legalservices/lris/directory.html* for a list of three hundred lawyer referral services across the country, including all those certified by the ABA.

• If you hire a lawyer on the Web and want to confirm that he or she is admitted to the bar, visit the ABA's directory of state bar admission offices at *www.abanet.org/legaled/baradmissions/ barcont.html*.

- For a listing of all state and major local bar associations with an Internet presence, visit the website of the ABA's Division for Bar Services at *www.abanet.org/barserv/stlobar.html*.
- To find legal services for the poor in your area, contact your bar association or look in the Yellow Pages under "Legal Aid" or "Legal Services." For a listing of legal-service programs for the poor in every state, access the directory of the ABA's Division for Legal Services at *www.abanet.org/legalservices/probono/directory .html*.
- Links to legal-aid and legal-services sites providing legal information for each state can be found at *www.ptla.org/links.htm*.
- Visit *www.lsc.gov/fundprog.htm* to learn about programs in all states funded by the federal Legal Services Corporation.
- If you're interested in doing some legal work yourself, some referral services will refer clients to lawyers who are willing to unbundle services. Visit *www.findlegalhelp.org* for more information.
- To make a complaint about your lawyer, call your state bar association, which will tell you how to proceed, or visit *www .abanet.org/cpr/disciplinary.html* for a listing of lawyer disciplinary agencies in every state.
- The ABA Division for Legal Services provides information about resolving disputes with your lawyer, and links to websites on mediation, arbitration, and disciplinary action, at *www .findlegalhelp.org*.
- The ABA Roadmaps Series can provide you with valuable information about representing yourself in court. Check out *Litigants Without Lawyers* and *User-Friendly Courts*. All titles are listed at *www.abanet.org/justice/roadmaps.html*.

REMEMBER THIS

- If you are involved in a dispute, it doesn't automatically mean you need a lawyer. Keep an open mind and be aware of all your options. If you're not sure what to do, seek legal advice.

- If your dispute is serious, if someone has commenced legal action against you, or if you're injured, see a lawyer without delay. Getting advice early could save you time and money.
- It's worth spending some time to find a lawyer who is appropriately qualified and right for you. You may have to interview more than one lawyer to find the right match.
- Don't be afraid to ask your prospective lawyer questions—your lawyer is there to help you!
- If things don't turn out the way you'd hoped, discuss your concerns with your lawyer. He or she might be able to explain what happened in a way that makes sense to you.
- If you have serious concerns about your lawyer's conduct, don't be afraid to pursue the matter through your state disciplinary authority.

CHAPTER 8

Where Do You Go from Here?

Our Top Recommendations for Further Resources

A NOTE FROM THE EDITORS AT THE ABA

We've provided you with a great deal of information in this book, but we're not ready for our swan song just yet. We've compiled a list of even more resources for you to check out. (A few of these may have been mentioned in previous chapters, but we still think they're the best places for you to start.)

FOUR WEBSITES TO GET YOU STARTED

These websites feature lengthy sections on topics associated with negotiation, mediation, arbitration, and court procedures. You're bound to find what you're looking for at one of these sites, or from one of the links these sites provide.

The American Bar Association Section of Dispute Resolution
www.abanet.org/dispute/home.html
The American Bar Association's Section of Dispute Resolution offers free publications covering negotiation, mediation, and arbitration in all their forms.

The Program on Negotiation at Harvard Law School
www.pon.org
The Program on Negotiation at Harvard Law School is a one-stop shop for information about negotiation and conflict

resolution. Its website offers a list of further resources available in its online clearinghouse.

FindLaw for the Public
http://public.findlaw.com/adr/
The FindLaw website features articles, FAQs, and links to further information relating to mediation and arbitration.

FreeAdvice.com
http://law.freeadvice.com/litigation/
The FreeAdvice website features information about alternatives to litigation and basic information about litigation procedure.

A NOVEL IDEA:
READ MORE ABOUT IT

Each of the books listed below makes for informative and valuable reading. These are just a few titles with which to start, on a variety of topics relating to dispute resolution. Don't forget to check out the offerings at your local library, and at *Amazon.com* and other online bookstores.

Getting to Yes: Negotiating Agreement Without Giving In, by Bruce Patton, Roger Fisher and William Ury (2nd edition, Penguin Books, 1991), is an excellent introduction to negotiating all kinds of disputes.

Difficult Conversations: How to Discuss What Matters Most, by Douglas Stone, Sheila Heen, Roger Fisher, and Bruce Patton (Penguin, 1999), focuses on negotiation in the context of interpersonal disputes. It provides information and advice about how to negotiate effectively when interpersonal relationships are involved.

Everybody's Guide to Small Claims Court, by Ralph Warner (7th edition, Nolo, 1997), provides information for people who are representing themselves in small-claims court.

DON'T FORGET

While websites and books are great places to obtain information, you might also want to check out any local venues offering courses, lectures and seminars, or expert panels relating to the topic of dispute resolution. Check with your local library, bar association, college, senior citizens' center, or hospital (to name just a few possible venues) to see if anything is in the works. Your local radio and TV stations might also offer some salient programming.

And don't forget about the countless posting boards, user groups, mailing lists, and chat rooms that exist on the Internet. Many of these could help you in your quest for knowledge and/or provide a network of support, depending on the issues you're facing. Communicating with others who have been in your position is a great way to learn about other avenues to explore, and what pitfalls to avoid.

We hope we've provided you with enough information to get you started, and we welcome your comments and suggestions for future editions of this book. Please visit us on the Web at *www .abanet.org/publiced/* or drop us a line via e-mail at *abapubed@ abanet.org.*

INDEX

abbreviated award, 89

administrative agencies, redress through, 128–129

Administrative Law Judge (ALJ), 129

admissibility of evidence, 144

admissions, 136–137

advisory arbitration, 81

Age Discrimination in Employment Act, 74

American Arbitration Association (AAA), 16, 68, 87, 91

American Bar Association (ABA)
directory of state bar admission offices, 173
Division for Bar Services, 174
Division for Legal Services, 174
Division for Public Education, 16, 151
Roadmaps Series, 174
Section of Dispute Resolution, 16, 176

American Bar Association Family Legal Guide (book), 173

anchoring (making first negotiation offer), 36–37

answer (defendant's response to complaint), 135–137

appeals
civil court litigation, 148
small-claims court, 112–114

arbitration
advisory arbitration, 81
arbitrator, selection of, 84–86
arbitrators' expertise, 82–83
arbitrators' immunity from lawsuits, 75

award (arbitrator's decision), 83, 87, 89

benefits of, 75, 77–83

binding arbitration, 9, 10–11, 71

class action suits and, 76

Code of Ethics for Arbitrators in Commercial Disputes, 84–85, 91

confidentiality and, 80–81

contexts in which arbitration is used, 68

contract-based mandatory arbitration, 70–72, 73, 74, 76–77, 87, 88–89

court-ordered arbitration, 70

defining characteristics, 67

in employment contexts, 72, 73, 74

enforcement of decisions, 82

enforcement of rights through, 77–78

finality of decisions, 81–82

final-offer arbitration, 70

grievance arbitration, 72

history of, 69

how cases get to arbitration, 69–72

interest-based arbitration, 72, 78

judge-arbitrator comparison, 86

jurisdictional considerations, 83

jury avoidance through, 83

laws regarding, 72, 75

for lawyers' disputes with clients, 161

mediation, comparison with, 67–68

arbitration (*cont'd*)
  negotiation, comparison with, 67–68
  nonbinding arbitration, 9, 81
  overview of, 9–11
  pendulum arbitration, 70
  precedent and, 79–80
  process of, 86–87, 89
  resources on, 85, 90–91
  rule-setting for, 86–87, 88
  tips to remember, 91–92
  vacating arbitrator's decision, 89–90
  voluntary arbitration, 69–70
Association for Conflict Resolution, 41, 65
attorney-client privilege, 138, 166, 171
attorneys, *see* lawyers
award (arbitrator's decision), 83, 87, 89

bench trial, 144
best alternative to a negotiated agreement (BATNA), 24–26, 27, 31, 34
"beyond a reasonable doubt" standard of proof, 120
bidding against yourself, 37
binding arbitration, 9, 10–11, 71
Brown v. Board of Education, 127–128
Burger, Warren, 75, 77

Caley v. Gulfstream, 74
cancelled checks as evidence, 105
Carnival Cruise Lines v. Shute, 88–89
case in chief, 144
caucusing, 54–55
charge to the jury, 146–147
civil court litigation, 117, 119
  administrative alternatives, 128–129

answer (defendant's response to complaint), 135–137
appeals, 148
behavior in court, 141
closing arguments, 146
complaint, filing of, 132–134, 135
courthouse environment, 118
decision on whether to file lawsuit, 122–129
default judgment, 136
defendant, identifying and locating, 130–131
defining characteristics, 119–120
discovery (fact-finding process), 137–138, 139
enforcement of judgment, 148–150
evidence for, 123, 144–146
examination of witnesses, 144–146
frivolous lawsuits, 122
grounds for lawsuit, determination of, 122–123
hurdles to filing lawsuit, 130
initiating a lawsuit, 129–131
injunctions, 119, 126
judge *vs.* jury trials, 144
judgment on verdict, 148
jurisdiction of court and, 131
jury deliberations, 147
jury instructions, 146–147
jury selection, 142–143
lawyers and, 132
"liable" judgment against losers, 119–120
objections during trial, 145
opening statements, 143–144
overview of, 14–16
parties to litigation, 121
personal effects on litigants, 127
precedent and, 127–128
pretrial conference, 138

pretrial procedures, 132–139
public nature of, 61–62
remedies, 125–126
resources on, 151
service of process, 134
settlement conference,
    138–139, 140
standards of proof, 120, 141
statute of limitations and,
    124–125
trial, 139–148
typical civil court cases,
    121–122
verdict, 147–148
claim for relief, 133, 135
class action suits, 76
client assistance funds, 173
client indemnity funds, 173
client security funds, 173
closing arguments, 146
collaborative law, 41
Collaborative Law Center, 41
co-mediation, 6
Commonwealth Coatings Corp. v.
    Continental Casualty Co., 90
compensatory damages, 125
complaints, filing of
  administrative cases, 128–129
  civil court litigation, 132–134,
    135
  lawyers, complaints against,
    171–173, 174
  small-claims court, 101–102
confidentiality
  arbitration and, 80–81
  lawyers and, 171
  mediation and, 61–63
conflict, 1–2
contingency fees, 60, 163–165
contracts
  arbitration clauses, 70–72, 73,
    74, 76–77, 87, 88–89
  as evidence in small-claims
    court, 105

negotiation and, 3
  oral contracts, 105
counterclaims, 102, 103
counteroffers, 37–38
counts, 135
county courts, 94
courthouse environment, 118
Court of Arbitration for Sport, 67,
    79, 83, 90
court of common pleas, 94
court-ordered arbitration, 70
creative problem solving
  mediation and, 58–59
  negotiation and, 34–35
credibility of a witness, 145
criminal courts, 14, 119, 120
cross-examination, 145

damages, 125–126
default judgment, 112, 136
defendants, 121
depositions, 115, 137–138
direct examination, 145
discovery (fact-finding process),
    137–138, 139
district court, 94
divorce mediation, 6–7

enforcement officers, 149
engagement letters, 154
Equal Employment Opportunity
    Commission (EEOC), 5,
    128
ERISA, 74
estates, 121–122
evaluative mediation, 48
evidence
  in civil court litigation, 123,
    144–146
  in small-claims court, 104–108
examination of witnesses, 144–146
expert witnesses, 105
eyewitnesses, 104–105, 106,
    107–108

facilitative mediation, 47
Fair Labor Standards Act, 74
family law, 45, 121
Federal Arbitration Act (FAA) of
    1925, 69, 72, 75, 89, 90
final-offer arbitration, 70
fixed fees, 165–166
"for cause" concept, 142
frivolous lawsuits, 122

general jurisdiction courts, 131
Getting to Yes (Patton et al.), 24,
    40, 177
grievance arbitration, 72
"guilty" concept, 119

income execution, 149
injunctions, 119, 126
interest-based arbitration, 72, 78
interests (negotiator's personal
    stake in outcome), 22–24,
    32, 34
International Association of Profes-
    sional Debt Arbitrators, 85
International Chamber of Com-
    merce, 68
International Institute for Conflict
    Prevention and Resolution,
    91
interrogatories in aid of execution,
    115

judges
    Administrative Law Judge (ALJ),
        129
    arbitrators, comparison with, 86
    judge vs. jury trials, 144
    mediators, comparison with, 64
judgment debtor, 148
judgment on verdict, 148
judgment-proof persons, 97, 126,
    150
jurisdictional limit on amount of
    money sought, 96–97

jurisdiction of court, 131
jury deliberations, 147
jury duty, 143
jury instructions, 146–147
jury selection, 142–143
jury vs. judge trials, 144
justice of the peace courts, 12

lawsuits, see civil court litigation
lawyers, 152
    advertising by, 161
    arbitration of disputes with
        clients, 161
    attorney-client privilege, 138,
        166, 171
    billing arrangements, 162
    civil court litigation and, 132
    client's responsibilities toward
        lawyer, 170
    communication with clients, 169
    competence concerns, 169
    complaint against a lawyer, filing
        of, 171–173, 174
    confidentiality and, 171
    conflict of interest concerns,
        171
    costs of legal representation, 60,
        154, 160, 161–167, 170
    decision on whether to hire a
        lawyer, 152–155
    diligence responsibility of, 169
    disciplinary actions against, 167
    ethical obligations of, 123,
        167–171
    fees charged by, 162–166
    finding a lawyer, 155–161
    firing a lawyer, 172
    following client's instructions,
        responsibility for, 169
    government lawyers who help
        general public, 157–159
    hiring a lawyer, 154, 159–161
    limited scope of representation,
        157

litigation lawyers, 158
low-cost legal help, 157, 174
malpractice suits against, 173
mediation and, 56, 60
mediation of disputes with
  clients, 161
meeting with your prospective
  lawyer, 159–161
money or property of client,
  guidelines for holding, 171,
  173
negotiation and, 20
as preventers of legal problems,
  155
referral services regarding, 156,
  173
resources on, 173–174
retainers charged by, 166
saving on legal costs, 165,
  166–167
small-claims court and, 95–96
talking to your lawyer, tips on,
  168
transactional lawyers, 158
unbundled legal services, 157,
  174
legal-aid programs, 157, 174
legal representation, *see* lawyers
Legal Services Corporation, 174
letters as evidence, 105
"liable" judgment against trial
  losers, 119–120
liens, 150
limited scope of representation, 157
litigation, *see* civil court litigation
litigation lawyers, 158

magistrate's courts, 12, 94–95
malpractice suits against lawyers,
  173
mediation
  agreement stage, 55–56
  appropriate and inappropriate
    cases for, 6–7, 44

arbitration, comparison with,
  67–68
caucusing, 54–55
certification for mediators, 49
choosing a mediator, 49, 51
co-mediation, 6
confidentiality and, 61–63
courts' requirements for, 52
creative problem solving, 58–59
defining characteristics, 43
dialogue between parties, 54
divorce mediation, 6–7
enforcement of agreements, 56,
  57
evaluative mediation, 48
facilitation services for, 51
facilitative mediation, 47
history of, 46
judges and mediators, comparison of, 64
lawyers and, 56, 60
for lawyers' disputes with
  clients, 161
mediator's role, 43, 47–51
memorandum of understanding,
  6–7, 55
money savings with, 60
as negotiation alternative, 39
opening statements of mediator
  and parties, 53–54
outlining the nature of dispute,
  53
overview of, 4–9
peer mediators, 8
private *vs.* public resolution of
  disputes, 46
process of, 53–56
pros and cons of, 57–65
relationship preservation
  through, 57–58
resources on, 65–66
restorative justice programs,
  50
in schools, 8

mediation (*cont'd*)
  settlement, legal ramifications
    of, 56
  settlement conference and, 63,
    139
  shuttle diplomacy, 6, 54–55
  as small-claims court alterna-
    tive, 98
  talking about problems related
    to case, opportunity for, 61
  time savings with, 60
  tips to remember, 66
  training for mediators, 48–49,
    65
  transformative mediation, 48
  types of disputes using media-
    tion, 45
  as voluntary process, 45
  ways in which disputes get to
    mediation, 51–52
  winning a case and, 63–65
memorandum of understanding,
  6–7, 55

National Arbitration Forum, 91
National Association for Community Mediation, 65
National Consumer Law Center, 91
National Grain and Feed Association, 79
National Labor Relations Board,
  128
National Working Rights Institute,
  83
negotiation, 18–19
  anchoring (making the first
    offer), 36–37
  arbitration, comparison with,
    67–68
  aversion of negotiation, ways to
    overcome, 36
  best alternative to a negotiated
    agreement (BATNA), 24–26,
    27, 31, 34

bidding against yourself, 37
collaborative law, 41
contracts and, 3
counteroffers, 37–38
creative problem solving, 34–35
decision whether or not to negotiate, 19–21
defining characteristics, 3
difficult negotiator, dealing with,
  38–39
difficult questions, handling of,
  33
enforcing a negotiated agreement, 39–40
independent advice regarding,
  21
interests (negotiator's personal
  stake in outcome), 22–24,
  32, 34
lawyers and, 20
location for, 35
mediation as alternative to, 39
other party, evaluation of, 31–34
overview of, 2–4
position (point of view during
  negotiation), 22–24
power differentials between negotiators, 37
preparing for, 21–35, 40
process of, 35–38
reactive devaluation, 27
reservation point (negotiator's
  walk-away point), 20, 29–31
resources on, 40–41
salary negotiation, 30
self-assessment for, 22–31
targets (outcomes negotiators
  want to achieve), 20, 26–29,
  31
third-party figures influencing
  the situation, 32
tips to remember, 42
winner's curse, 28
win-win outcomes, 34–35

wrong person, negotiating with, 32
nominal damages, 126
nonbinding arbitration, 9, 81
North American Free Trade Agreement (NAFTA), 68

objections during trial, 145
opening statements
    civil court litigation, 143–144
    mediation, 53–54
oral contracts, 105

participation agreements, 41
peer mediators, 8
pendulum arbitration, 70
peremptory challenges, 142
personal-injury disputes, 122
personal property, seizure of, 150
petitioners, 121
photographs as evidence, 105
plaintiffs, 121
position (point of view during negotiation), 22–24
power differentials between negotiators, 37
prayer for relief, 134
precedent
    arbitration and, 79–80
    civil court litigation and, 127–128
"preponderance of the evidence" standard of proof, 120, 141
presiding juror, 147
pretrial conference, 138
process servers, 134
procuring cause, 83
pro se courts, 12
punitive damages, 125–126

reactive devaluation, 27
reasoned award, 89
receipts as evidence, 105

remedies in civil court litigation, 125–126
reservation point (negotiator's walk-away point), 20, 29–31
respondents, 121
restorative justice programs, 50
retainer fees, 166
retainers, 166
right-to-sue letters, 129

salary negotiation, 30
schools' use of mediation, 8
service procedures (notifying a defendant)
    civil court litigation, 134
    small-claims court, 102–104
settlement, legal ramifications of, 56
settlement conference, 63, 138–139, 140
shuttle diplomacy, 6, 54–55
small-claims court, 93
    appeals, 112–114
    cases suitable for, 96–99
    collecting an award, 114–115
    complaint form, filing of, 101–102
    counterclaims, 102, 103
    default judgment against defendant, 112
    enforcement of judgment, 13
    evidence in, 104–108
    failure to appear in court, consequences of, 112
    hearing before a judge, 108–111
    judgment-proof persons and, 97
    jurisdictional limit on amount of money sought, 96–97
    laws regarding, 94–95
    lawyers and, 95–96
    mediation as alternative to, 98
    names of courts in different regions, 12
    overview of, 11–14

small-claims court (*cont'd*)
  preparing a case, 104–108,
    109–111
  procedures in, 100–104
  resources on, 115–116
  service procedures (notifying a
    defendant), 102–104
  state regulation of, 94–95
  statute of limitations and, 100
  tax court, 95
  where to bring a case, 99–100
special jurisdiction courts, 131
specific performance, orders for,
    126
standards of proof, 120, 141
statute of limitations, 100,
    124–125
summons, 134
superior court, 94
Supreme Court, 89, 90, 127–128

targets (outcomes negotiators want
    to achieve), 20, 26–29, 31
tax court, 95
time-barred lawsuits, 124

transactional lawyers, 158
transformative mediation, 48
trial court of general jurisdiction,
    94
trial de novo, 112
trial procedures, 139–148

unbundled legal services, 157, 174
Uniform Arbitration Act (UAA) of
    1955, 75
Uniform Mediation Act, 49

verdicts, 147–148
Victim-Offender Mediation
    (VOM), 50
voir dire, 142
voluntary arbitration, 69–70

wage garnishment, 149
wills, 121–122
winner's curse, 28
win-win outcomes, 34–35
"without prejudice" concept, 55
World Anti-Doping Agency, 83

ABOUT THE AUTHOR

Sheila M. Maloney is the Assistant Director of the Program on Negotiation and Mediation at Northwestern University School of Law. She teaches courses in interest-based negotiation principles and skills. She is also a mediator, and serves on the Board of Directors at the Center for Conflict Resolution.

Prior to joining the faculty at Northwestern University School of Law, Ms. Maloney worked as a business litigation attorney in Chicago, Illinois, advocating for clients in litigation, arbitration and mediation contexts.

Ms. Maloney received her Bachelor's degree in English from the University of Illinois and her Juris Doctor from Northwestern University School of Law. She is an active member of the American Bar Association's Section of Dispute Resolution, the Association for Conflict Resolution, and the Hispanic Lawyers Association of Illinois.